THE ART OF
COUNSELLING AND
PSYCHOTHERAPY

THE ART OF
COUNSELLING AND
PSYCHOTHERAPY

Rainer Matthias Holm-Hadulla

Translated from German by
Andrew Jenkins

KARNAC
LONDON   NEW YORK

Published in 2004 by
H. Karnac (Books) Ltd.
6 Pembroke Buildings, London NW10 6RE

This revised and expanded English edition is based on the earlier edition in German published by Verlag Vandenhoek & Ruprecht Die Psychotherapeutische Kunst in 1997.

British Library Cataloguing in Publication Data

A C.I.P. for this book is available from the British Library

ISBN 1 85575 946 2

Edited, designed, and produced by The Studio Publishing Services Ltd, Exeter EX4 8JN

Printed in Great Britain

10 9 8 7 6 5 4 3 2 1

www.karnacbooks.com

CONTENTS

"Such shaping phantasies that apprehend
More than cool reason ever comprehends."
William Shakespeare, *A Midsummer Night's Dream*

ABOUT THE AUTHOR

Rainer Matthias Holm-Hadulla is a Professor at the University of Heidelberg. He is head of the Psychotherapeutic Counselling Centre for Students, and also works as a psychotherapist and analyst in private practice. His activities extend to the field of continuing education. In addition, he acts as a counsellor to executives and organizations. His main scientific interests are creativity, counselling, and psychotherapy.

FOREWORD

As always, it is a source of gratification to me when someone active in a particular branch of science can make meaningful use of my own contributions to philosophy. Attempting to understand others should be an aim recognized and respected by all those taking a conscientious attitude to the challenges posed by their own field of scholarship or science.

In addition, I find it very gratifying that this book has a wide readership, and I hope and believe that the second edition will broaden that audience and bring the author the confirmation he so richly deserves.

Hans Georg Gadamer

CHAPTER ONE

Introduction and overview

Personal, social, or vocational problems may be serious enough to prompt some people to seek professional advice. Some may start having doubts about their personal development and sign up for seminars. Others consult therapists because they are aware of their own inhibitions, anxieties, or depressive moods. Alongside the help they need to deal with the more or less clearly defined problems or symptoms they have, they are all seeking three things: competent guidance in connection with their personal development, expert assistance in coping productively with professional and social challenges, and dependable support in making a success of their lives.

This book is, on the one hand, about preventing and coping with psychic problems. But it is also about how to discover one's personal abilities and creative potential. It sets out to show how counselling and psychotherapy can release the creativity most people have, and how they can improve the quality of their personal and social lives.

The central issue involved in personal and social development is creative authenticity. Being creative and authentic means assuming authorship of one's own life. This is why the objective rules of counselling and psychotherapy have to be supplemented by a practical, subjective component that can guide counsel-seekers, clients, and patients in their endeavour to achieve personal authorship.

At first it may seem strange to use the term "creative" with reference to the handling and management of personal and vocational relations. Although it is a view that is essentially implicit in the practice of counselling and psychotherapy, there is frequently uncertainty about how creativity should be understood, and how it can be actively encouraged. In the course of this book we shall see that creativity is a permanent challenge, a specific attitude to life. This, in its turn, implies that crises are not merely setbacks or disruptions, but existentially significant experiences that can further personal maturity and growth. It is eternally fascinating to observe how some people are able to master crises and use them as stepping-stones to a "higher" form of health, while in others similar crises lead to a lasting impairment of their *élan vital*, to boredom, futility, and despair. Many counsellors and psychotherapists emphasize the importance of individual creativity; many artists and scientists have testified to the healing effect of creative activity. This book extends that perspective to encompass everyday creativity as a necessary component of an art of living that actively precludes the very onset of psychic disorders.

One of the essential conditions for success in mastering this art of living is the ability that most of us have to cope creatively with difficult experiences by the force of our imagination. As we shall see, this kind of creativity is not bound up with any special gift of an artistic nature.

The creative ability to cope with difficult experiences in our lives is something that counselling and psychotherapy can and should systematically enhance. The duration, profundity, and complexity of these problems will determine whether it will take a few sessions or a long course of treatment to initiate an internal development process that prevents or remedies the withdrawal into anxiety, depression, addiction, and other psychic disorders.

The guiding principle of counselling and therapy is to initiate or encourage a creative psychic engagement with the things we experience in life. This is of major significance in linking immediate experience with constructive understanding. In our modern scientific and technological age, authentic and creative experience of reality is doubly indispensable if our psychic capacities are not to capitulate in the face of the strains placed on them by crude, atomizing materialism and the gradual loss of consistent values.

The main concern of this book is to establish a creative attitude in counselling and psychotherapy. One factor of central moment for a creative attitude, as for counselling and psychotherapy in general, is the quality of the helping relationship.

The helping relationship or alliance is a special form of human encounter. That encounter involves two (or more) persons, each with their own individual history. As in any other kind of encounter, they will seek to establish communicative ground upon which they can genuinely hope to achieve understanding. Counsel-seekers and patients will normally organize their personal and social histories in the way that an author organizes a narrative. This "authorship" gives them the feeling of personal agency which, in its turn, affords new perspectives on their life situation. This is by no means restricted to individual biography. Stories have always been important for the people who feel the need to tell them. But they also establish and enhance social community. They are handed down to others in oral and written forms, or in ritual enactment; they live on in customs, fairy tales, lore and legend, movies, everyday language. They find their highest and most coherent form in art and religion. My attempt to understand these constant companions of our lives centres on a belief in the creativity of "communicative existence". I use this term to express the fact that we are in a permanent state of external and internal dialogue with others and ourselves. Engaging fully in that dialogue can help us solve many of our problems and master our psychic conflicts.

The dialogues of Socrates show that the positive influence of "beautiful conversations" is not based on suggestion and hocus-pocus. Such dialogic exchanges are rationally plausible ways of strengthening personal development, solving social and political problems, and resolving psychic conflicts. Plato rails against charlatans who use sorcery and mumbo-jumbo to solve problems, alleviate mental distress, and heal the sick. For Plato, counselling and psychological advice are only legitimate if in both content and form they explicitly centre on the individuality of the client (see Gadamer, 1991). Later, Hippocrates declared this kind of counselling and psychotherapy to be an essential and indispensable part of the art of healing. But the Greeks were also fully sensible to the problems involved in distinguishing clearly between rationally conducted psychotherapeutic counselling and the deliberately arcane, if not downright fraudulent, practices of self-styled faith healers. Even today, 2,000 years later, we are still haunted by the question of what it is precisely that distinguishes the salutary and beneficial "beautiful conversation" from the insult to the rational self represented by the posturings and antics of the charlatan.

The word "charlatan" itself reflects the ambiguity inherent in the idea of helping through speech. *Charlare* has the meaning of "telling stories", "influencing", "treating with words". Thus, on the one hand, a charlatan is one who cures by telling stories. Our usage of the word today, however, invariably implies the idea of a swindler or impostor. For some scientists the concept of healing by speech is so suspect that they advocate an approach to psychology and psychotherapy modelled on the natural sciences and closely monitored by experimentation and mathematical proofs. While this has the advantage of producing precise statistics and verifiable hypotheses, it does nothing to elucidate or illuminate the emotional and charismatic elements of counselling and therapeutic interviews.

However, the intrinsic ambiguity inherent in the idea of helping by speech as identified by the ancient Greeks is merely a special instance of the ambiguity involved in all human communication. We know how fine the dividing line can be between understanding and misunderstanding, between cogency and casuistry, exhortation and rabble-rousing, persuasion and sedition. Language itself refuses to be submitted to the confines of precise definition. In living usage, the expressions we use are invariably related to the situation in which we use them and are dependent on the cooperation of the addressee if they are to be properly understood. As Weinrich (1974) points out, if I pronounce the word "fire" out of the blue, no one will know what I mean. In a process of abstraction, a scientist may eliminate the context of my statement and activate the definition of "fire" as a state of combustion in which inflammable material burns, producing heat, flames, and smoke. But he will still not know what I meant. How much easier—and how much richer—is the understanding of the word in a concrete situation, for example, if I come running out of the house in a state of disarray, loudly exclaiming the word "Fire!"

Given the situational nature of speech, generations of thinkers have tussled with the problem of how we can tell what is true from what is untrue. None of them has advanced beyond Wittgenstein's (1953) laconic statement that the truth of an utterance depends on the use made of it by participants in a language game. Accordingly, if one person can make use of another person's utterances to expand his or her own horizon, then they are true. It is in this way that understanding comes about.

This pragmatic view of communication is asserting itself more and more widely. Its insights are of major importance not only in linguistics but also in our social lives and in the political context. Leading European and American thinkers like Jürgen Habermas (1971) and Richard Rorty (2001) regard "communicative reason" and "communicative action" as the very foundation of democratic communities.

In the modern age, there can be no doubt of the pioneering role played by psychoanalysis in dealing with personal problems and psychic disorders by means of communicative action. The guiding conviction of psychoanalysis is the feasibility of solving problems, removing disorders, and improving the quality of a person's life by inducing awareness of repressed psychic urges in the framework of confidential verbal exchanges. The impact of psychoanalysis on the intellectual life of the last century was unrivalled by any other form of psychology. Impassioned advocates and vitriolic critics have engaged in controversies of such acrimony that it is difficult to preserve the intellectual and therapeutic substance of this theory of the nature of the human mind, social relationships, and psycho-therapeutic treatment.

In recent years, we have seen an increasing disinclination in the literature on scientifically oriented counselling and therapy to polarize the different techniques in use (and frequently to give distorted accounts of rival approaches in the process). Summarizing developments over past decades, Jerome Frank (1991) concludes that today most practitioners are client- and patient-orientated rather than method-orientated. For all the advantages this has, there are also drawbacks, notably the tendency towards an inchoate poly-pragmatism in counselling and psychotherapy. Both the interested public and inexperienced counsellors and therapists need guidelines if they are not to lose their bearings in the emotional processes set in train by counselling and therapy. On the other hand, such guidelines may all too easily congeal into dogmatic stances estranged from the realities of life.

Dissatisfaction with the eclectic commingling of counselling and therapy techniques, on the one hand, and awareness of the necessity of making discriminating use of different techniques to achieve optimal counselling and treatment results on the other, have stimulated a broad range of efforts to achieve an integrative approach to counselling and psychotherapy. In a bid to live up to the claims of being "scientific," attempts to derive general principles for integrative counselling and therapy from empirical studies are increasingly common. But even "evidence-based" counselling and therapy techniques are ultimately products of pre-scientific, "natural" methods of counselling and treatment. The collected wisdom of generations and the fruits of a long history of ideas will necessarily leave their imprint, even on the most "objective" counselling and therapy methods. Vice versa, established scientific knowledge has an undeniable impact on the culture of everyday life. Looking briefly at the conclusions modern psychotherapy research draws from its studies (see, e.g., Lambert, 2004), we can identify five central areas common to the individual counselling and therapy schools, albeit with differing emphasis:

- establishing a helping relationship
- insight into problems and conflicts
- strengthening of selfhood and self-efficacy
- enhancement of interpersonal relations
- actualization of resources

Establishing a helping relationship

The importance of the personal relationship for the success of counselling and treatment is more or less axiomatic. As we all know, the same message pronounced by a priest, teacher, or doctor will have a different effect. But for enlightened minds committed to the principles of perspicuity and common sense, charismatic influences and effects are a problematic phenomenon. Accordingly, in counselling and therapy as elsewhere, the quest for objective techniques largely independent of personal influences has long been high on the agenda.

It was in the late nineteenth century that, in the wake of the initial triumphs of an objectifying, scientific approach to medicine, therapists began treating mental and psychological ailments on a scientific basis. The first technique to be developed was hypnosis. With this method Josef Breuer attempted to cure his patient " Anna O." (in reality Berta von Pappenheim, later a prominent figure in the women's rights movement), whose symptoms included hallucinations, fits, paralysis, and disorganized speech. He was surprised by the subjective factor that materialized in the course of treatment. When Breuer found he was not making any progress, he referred the patient to Freud for further therapy. Freud identified the role played by the patient's relationship with the therapist. It represented a recapitulation of earlier relational patterns that had left their mark on the patient's life. On the basis of this and other observations, Freud's successors elevated the analysis of the relationship with the therapist to the pivotal factor in psychoanalytic therapy. This emphasis on the subjective relationship with the counsellor or therapist was bound to be regarded as a challenge to the ideal of objectivity upheld by those psychotherapy researchers who accused psychoanalysis of being unscientific. It triggered a quest for techniques devoid of any kind of dependence on the nature of the personal relationship between patient and therapist. Ultimately, however, it transpired that even the proponents of so objective and scientific an approach as behavioural therapy had to concede that the specific quality of the patient–therapist relationship is of decisive significance for treatment success. Accordingly, modern counselling and therapy is geared to giving the subjective nature of the helping relationship its due without lapsing into personal prejudice. In the following, I shall accordingly concentrate on the subjective factor operative in counselling and psychotherapy, while at the same time indicating objective criteria that can be drawn upon to verify the value and coherence of psychotherapeutic interventions.

Insight into problems and conflicts

As it is part of our human condition to be "concealed from ourselves," we need communication partners if we are to engage in a productive form of self-reflection. So it is frequently the task of the counsellor or therapist to engage in a respectful analysis and understanding of the problems and conflicts presented to him or her. Here, different schools of thought have chosen very different approaches. Take the example of clients prompted to seek counselling or therapy by the fear of failing to achieve social recognition. They feel despised, have little self-confidence, are dogged by feelings of inadequacy. But the counselling interviews reveal that in their social, and above all professional, surroundings they behave impeccably. In contrast to their assessment of themselves, colleagues confirm the quality of their work and even express a degree of annoyance at the lack of self-assurance they display.

What can insight into problems and conflicts mean in such a context? After analysing their behaviour, one could of course offer such clients a training programme designed to improve their social skills and bolster their self-assurance. But what strategy is the right one if, in more in-depth exchanges, they admit that they have problems in their personal relationships, recoil at displays of physical affection from their partners, and feel generally unhappy? In such a situation, training in social skills might lead to better ways of coping with the problem while at the same time reinforcing the unconscious conflict. Then it would at all events be more appropriate to work on the repressed fantasies underlying their inability to engage in an intensive caring relationship, although that is precisely what they long for. Only a true understanding of the wishes and creative potentialities of the client or patient can provide the basis for a decision on the specific counsel or therapy focus suitable in each individual case.

Strengthening selfhood and self-efficacy

The offer of counselling or the acceptance of a patient for psychotherapy is enough to generate hope in the client or patient. This hope may be founded on liking and trust, the counsellor's reputation, or the therapist's professional qualifications. According to Jerome Frank (1991) and the findings of psychotherapy research in general, this is frequently an initial step towards overcoming the state of demoralization attendant upon many personal or work-related crises and psychic disorders. Once clients or patients begin to realize that they are able to join in shaping a therapeutic alliance, to reflect on their personal problems, and to understand their interpersonal relations, they will be reinforced in their feeling of selfhood and "self-efficacy" (Bandura, 1982).

Enhancement of interpersonal relations

Every client seeks positive feedback, every patient wants to be respected for what he or she really is. Counselling and therapy invariably activate feelings connected with interpersonal relations. Clients and patients do not engage with their relationships on an exclusively intellectual plane. They are quick to sense that their difficulties with other persons are bound up with conscious and unconscious emotions and fantasies, and that on their own they are unable to cope with these emotions and fantasies creatively. The empathic perception and understanding of unpleasant feelings related to interpersonal conflicts can be the decisive step in extricating oneself from moods of futility and despair. Success in shaping an emotionally significant world of ideas and fantasies is essential for living partnerships, whether of a private or professional nature. Here, it is of paramount importance for the counsellor or therapist to be able to accompany the client or patient into that world in a positive and strengthening way. This, in its turn, depends on his or her willingness and ability to achieve an actively creative approach to emotionally significant relationships.

Actualization of resources

Psychologically, the operative principle of resource activation brought to the fore by modern therapy research is again intuitively obvious. Common to all forms of professional counselling and therapy is the use of specific methods for discovering and strengthening the positive potential of clients and patients. Taking psychoanalysis and behavioural therapies as opposite poles, we can say that the former attempts to remove handicaps to the actualization of psychosocial resources by analysing the analytic relationship and biographically conditioned conflicts. Cognitive behavioural therapy addresses the resources directly, at a conscious level. The creative approach is characterized by the way it furthers personal and social resources by the active shaping of unconscious or not readily accessible ideas and fantasies.

Existing efforts to integrate different counselling and therapy techniques invite criticism for the way in which they frequently simplify traditions of thought and the insights produced by the various schools. Such simplifications appropriating ideas elaborated elsewhere and passing them off as the respective authors' own work are often motivated by academic or professional politics. Yet attempts to conceptualize counselling and therapy in terms of the integrative application of effective techniques are necessary. However loyal they may be to a particular school of thought, counsellors or therapists know that they have a whole range of possible interventions at their disposal, and that the relative appropriateness of those interventions will differ in each individual case. Here, a creative attitude can represent a cohesive humanistic foundation on which different counselling and therapy strategies can be applied individually.

To enlarge on the creative attitude as an essential counselling and therapy principle, I shall outline the idea of creativity in the next chapter, proceeding from there to illustrate its implications with reference to various cases of counselling and therapy. The subsequent chapters take a closer theoretical look at hermeneutics and aesthetics. But the more practically-minded reader can continue with the chapter on creative principles, while those particularly interested in counselling can move on to the chapter on counselling and coaching. The following chapters enlarge on the concept of the creative attitude in the field of brief dynamic and analytic psychotherapy. This leads into some reflections on the differences between professional relationships and "ordinary" relationships, and the ethical implications of the creative approach. The book closes with some thoughts on artistic shaping as a way of resolving psychic conflicts.

CHAPTER TWO

Creativity

We have pointed out that the "shaping of the helping relationship" plays a central role in very different approaches to counselling and therapy. The term "shaping" already suggests that this task has a creative aspect. Creativity itself, however, is a complex concept that is frequently used in a vague and ill-defined manner. In the following I shall acquaint the reader with some of its salient aspects.

In the most general sense, creativity is a characteristic of living beings, an everyday challenge, and a mysterious gift. Latin *creare* means "to bring about, give birth, bring to life". It is related to *crescere*: "to grow, take shape, come about, and let grow". In culture, science, economics, and politics, creativity is a much sought-after and highly valued characteristic. In the last few years, concepts like Csikszentmihalyi's "flow" (1996), with its emphasis on the playful, fun-oriented aspects of the creative personality and the creative process, have become highly influential in education and psychology. The concentration on fun and flow experiences is central in many approaches to parenting, encouragement for gifted children, leadership, counselling, and coaching. But there are also many accounts of the creative process that suggest that fun and flow are at best of secondary importance in this connection, and that self-oblivion, devotion to the matter in hand, and frustration tolerance are the main factors involved in productivity and creativity. A more profound understanding of creativity would seem to be necessary to encourage it by way of, say, counselling, coaching, and psychotherapy.

Culture–historical background of modern concepts of creativity

Mythologies of Creation in ancient civilizations are an excellent source of information on the culture-historical roots of modern creativity concepts. Indeed, we may legitimately regard them as religiously encoded theories of free subjectivity. Cultural historian and Egyptologist Jan Assmann (2000) describes how early human civilizations used myths of creation as a way of achieving and expressing an understanding of the complexion of reality and their place in it. In the cosmologies of ancient Egypt, the world was not created by one or more creator-gods or demiurges. It originated of its own accord. According to the mythologies of Heliopolis, the world came into being with the first rising of the sun, in which the self-created sun god emerged from the primal waters and sent out his rays into a world yet to take form and shape. Before this, there was nothing but lightless, endless, and formless chaos. In the ancient Egyptian view, Creation is never complete, it develops indefinitely and is repeated every morning anew. Creativity must assert itself against the permanent counter-pull exerted by chaos. The task of humankind is to participate in this unending process by means of rituals and daily work. Unlike the image of humanity in the Bible, the Egyptians believed they were fully and incessantly involved in the creative process. It was their duty to celebrate the sun and moon with hymns, to implore the risings of the Nile, to accompany sowing and harvesting with rituals, to hold animals sacred, to observe and preserve all cosmic and natural life with worshipful attention. All this expressed an awareness of human volition and striving as an integral part of the elemental processes taking their course in the natural and cosmic environment.

This aspect of ancient Egyptian creation mythology has all but disappeared from our modern western concepts of creativity. The modern mind sees creativity primarily in terms of innovation. This places it in opposition to nature. But for the ancient Egyptians creativity was a nature-bound form of behaviour that averted chaos and kept the world functioning.

The biblical image of creativity differs from that of the Egyptians in a number of essential ways that have a direct bearing on modern notions of what Creation means. The act of creation is performed by one single being. God acts in radical, unconditioned creativity and sovereignty. A second difference from the Egyptian view is the idea that creation took place at a definite point in time. However, since the Council of Trent we also have the notion of *creatio continua*, the ongoing activity of the Creator to ensure the maintenance and further development of the world. Third, the Bible presents the creation of the world as an act of creation *ex nihilo*. Heaven and earth came about through the act of creation and did not exist before. This audacious idea of making something from nothing has left its imprint on the ideas of western artists, scientists, entrepreneurs, and politicians about what it means to be creative.

There are major differences between biblical and Far Eastern notions of creativity. The idea of creation from nothing is entirely alien to Chinese thought. Here creativity is seen more as the transformation of something already there. Also, human creativity is described as analogous to nature, with many individuals participating in the creative process. By contrast, the concepts derived from biblical notions of creativity emphasize individuality and uniqueness. The great figures of the Renaissance—da Vinci, Michelangelo, Raphael—were regarded as universally educated original geniuses in the mould of the biblical creator-god. In the Renaissance the creative genius distinguished by originality and spontaneity became the quintessence of human self-actuation. The young Goethe also speaks of the genius as "divine," though in his classical period he was later to criticize the autonomy of genius as a loss of contact with reality, harmful to both the individual and society. Productive activity advances to the status of an equal substitute for genius. For the older Goethe, productivity, not genius, is the gauge of creative achievement.

In the latter part of the nineteenth century, genius achieves the cult status accorded to it by Friedrich Nietzsche and Richard

Wagner. The genius is allowed untrammelled licence, he is free to trample all over restrictive laws and limitations, even those imposed by nature. It was in this period that the cult of genius spread to other areas outside art; for example, in the adulation of a political figure like Napoleon. Leaders of totalitarian political systems profited from the increasing popularization of genius, taking it to such extremes of perversion in the later stages of the twentieth century that the very idea of genius gradually became obsolete. It was replaced in North America in the 1950s by the term "creativity". Creativity was now no longer regarded as the preserve of artists; it could be encountered in all walks of life.

Autobiographical accounts of creativity

A revealing source of enlightenment on the creative personality and the creative process is the life and work of Johann Wolfgang von Goethe. We have detailed accounts of his life from birth onward, and he himself describes his creative evolution in detail, from the games he played with dolls in his early years to the hours immediately before his death (see Friedenthal, 1963). Geniuses from other domains—Mozart, Picasso, Einstein—have, not surprisingly, left fewer testimonies of this kind, but what they do tell us shows a high degree of accord with Goethe's accounts.

For Goethe it was axiomatic that the talents and gifts we have are innate. But upbringing and the social environment decide whether that talent will come to fruition. Creativity has to have the right kind of family environment for it to develop. For Goethe, the enthusiasm of his mother and sister, the patient guidance given to him by his father, and the early break with his father's influence, were all of major significance.

Mozart, Goethe, Picasso, and Einstein all concur that creative labour is a serious business, they all refer to the feeling of being guided by a power outside themselves. A marked degree of self-oblivion and tenacity is indispensable for creative labour. All our geniuses were able to work under the most taxing conditions: deprivation, illness, danger to life and limb. When still a child, Mozart was astonishingly productive on the endless tours through Europe, full of discomfort and deprivation though they were.

Goethe went through a number of major psychological crises in both his youth and his adult life, but they never stopped him from working. In early infancy, Picasso was severely affected by the death of close relatives and the horrors of an earthquake, but this did nothing to quell his creative urge. Deprivation, illness, and menace contribute to the development of the creative personality and are exploited as a spur to creative activity. Despite deprivation, disappointment, and danger, creative personalities succeed in finding scope for their personal development in creative effort. Devotion to the self-imposed task in hand is described as exhausting, sometimes even actively threatening. Most creative people feel almost obsessed by an inexplicable urge to create. Different as they maybe in terms of personality, persuasions, and cultural affiliations, here they all agree.

Creativity differs greatly in different domains. Since Aristotle, the scientific mind has been notable for its objectivity and systematic strategic thinking. The scientific genius, says Schopenhauer, is supreme intellect plus perfect objectivity. By contrast, the artist is more volatile and subjective. The scientist must "deactivate" feelings, fantasies, and dreams, while for the artist close communion with the world of dream and imagination is highly beneficial. Scientists must restrict themselves patiently to an idea or a project and banish or divorce their individual sensibilities from the task in hand. These differences between creative personalities and creative activity in different domains are reflected in the lives led by the individuals involved.

Drawing some preliminary conclusions from these culture–historical and biographical testimonies (a more profound psychodynamic understanding of creativity will be outlined in the following chapters), we arrive at the following picture. Culture historians suggest that creative personalities respect natural and cultural life cycles. Although they may not see it this way themselves, creative personalities are integrated into a natural environment and a human community. The loneliness and self-centredness of "geniuses" may be the product of social standing (e.g. poverty and lack of recognition) rather than something inherent in creativity itself. Self-referentiality and isolation are more a characteristic of modern life styles than of the creative personality itself. The quest for hedonistic kicks and thrills is almost the exact opposite of creativity.

From a psychodynamic vantage, the impact of early socialization counts almost as much as individual talent. Creative people constantly stress how important the affection, interest, and encouragement of their parents were for their development. But equally there are accounts in which difficult, not to say disastrous, family backgrounds have acted as a spur for outstanding scientific, artistic, social, and political achievements. The bottom line appears to be that most productive and creative individuals contrive to see their personal fate realistically and attain an affirmative attitude. They find the scope they need to dedicate themselves to a particular task for its own sake. In this, passionate commitment, a capacity for play, and relatively high frustration tolerance are crucially significant.

Creativity is a natural characteristic of living beings and is not only found in extraordinary achievements. From a counselling and psychotherapeutic viewpoint, the development of one's own personality, the ability to sustain a meaningful relationship, the upbringing of children, and a positive attitude to ageing are all creative tasks. Psychic and interpersonal disturbances are typically bound up with a refusal to take an affirmative attitude to creative development and lifelong learning.

The virtues of the creative personality frequently go hand in hand with searing personal crises that demand to be respected as such. Thus, there can never be a uniform recipe for how best to encourage creativity. Parents, teachers, counsellors, and psychotherapists need to be aware of the multiplicity of creative conflicts if they are to provide effective aid in the discovery of creative potential and support for creative labour.

The following descriptions of cases of counselling and psychotherapy are designed as concrete illustrations of what I mean by a creative attitude. The subsequent reflection on hermeneutics and aesthetics sets out to place counselling and the psychotherapeutic interview on a sound epistemological foundation. Both describe the factors at work in general human exchange and, more specifically, in counselling and therapy. Common to both is the focus on creative processes that help people to find their way around the world they live in.

Cases of counselling and coaching are reported in Chapter Seven.

Three examples of counselling and psychotherapy

The relevance and cogency of case histories have been challenged frequently. One common criticism is that they trade too heavily on their aesthetic persuasiveness and as "narratives" fail to measure up to scientific criteria. But what kind of science are we dealing with if it refuses to admit the validity of impressions, feelings, and subjective experience? Take the wealth of inner experience we encounter when we read a fine novel. Such experience is "real" in the truest sense of the word: it has an effect; it helps. We could, of course, restrict ourselves to "genuinely" scholarly content analysis methods and use them to work out precisely how often, say, positive and negative ascriptions figure in the novel. But if we did so, we would be turning away from the full richness of experience afforded by the effect of the story on our imagination, the way it grips us, speaks to us, and shows us things in a new light. I have already indicated that aesthetic experience is not merely subjective and random. As cultural history shows, fine speech is more than mere gilding the lily. We need only recall the biblical figure of Joseph, or Sheherazade from *1001 Nights*, both of whom were able to free their lords from "psychological distemper" with the eloquence of their tales. Stories bring a different truth to light than the form of psychology that is orientated to statistical verification.

The names of patients featured in the following case histories have been changed to preserve their anonymity. Some of these histories have already appeared in scholarly journals in a slightly different form (see Holm-Hadulla, 1997).

Psychotherapeutic counselling

Robert, a 25-year-old student of literature, comes to me complaining of a feeling of "aimlessness" that has afflicted him for at least six months. Subject to strange bouts of "dizziness", he has already undergone neurological examination to rule out the suspicion of multiple sclerosis. His inability to devote himself to his studies has prompted him to think of leaving the university altogether. Constant brooding is stunting his intellectual potential and interfering with his freedom of mind, although he has always been an avid reader and fond of academic work. These problems are reflected in the poor grades he has been getting, and he is apprehensive about the outcome of his imminent exams. There are also conflicts of an ill-defined nature with his parents and problems with his sexuality. In the last few weeks he has been entertaining thoughts of suicide as a way of resolving these tensions and finding peace.

At this point Robert appears to have volunteered as much information as he is prepared to divulge. In view of the threatening nature of the patient's complaints and the necessity of swift crisis intervention, I attempt first of all to take the tension out of our exchange by creating a therapeutic space in which I can devote myself entirely to the patient's self-actuation. It strikes me that the tall, slim, physically striking young man is watching me closely with a mixture of defensiveness and anticipation, as if to say: "Right, that's my problem. Now it's your turn." I ask myself whether his controlled, walled-off, indeed actively rejective manner might not be designed to ensure that in the exchange between us our individual modes of viewing and experiencing things should be kept distinct as far as possible.

To gain time, I invite Robert to tell me more about himself. As he describes his present life situation, a visual impression suggests itself to me: "Robert is a cool, collected physician or priest with a penetrating stare that his little son cannot evade and that glues him to the spot."

Drawing on this visual image, I tell the patient that I have the impression that he is highly vigilant with respect to his own activities and treats himself very harshly and uncompromisingly. Robert responds to this intervention with interest and is clearly flattered, as if I had paid him a compliment. But then he reports that this impervious self-control he has imposed on himself has its price: the feeling of "living with the brakes on".

As I search for further internal images providing a key to Robert's emotional world, his tone suddenly changes. He begins to enlarge on the problematic aspects of the "physician with the piercing clinical gaze and the uncompromisingly righteous theologian", and plays through various scenarios in which his personal longings play a role. I have the impression that he is beginning to get closer to himself. Encouraged by my inquiries, he starts exploring his love life and reports on the way in which in puberty he felt that he must put himself on a tight rein so as not to "overstep the mark". The reasons he advances for this are first, that he is the son of a pietistic country doctor, and second, that he has two younger sisters, which meant that in early childhood he was allotted (and also accepted) the role of the sensible big brother telling his little sisters what to do. At this juncture, he makes reference to a more recent experience that casts light on the inhibition and hesitancy that were clearly not so marked in his childhood. At the age of twenty-one, following initial tentative attempts to make contact (including physical contact) with women and break away from his parents' sphere of influence, he fell passionately in love with a young woman. Their relationship lasted thirteen months. On the one hand, this was for him a fascinating, "terrific" experience, but it also had a darker side that he still finds oppressive and frightening. During their relationship the young woman suddenly developed massive anxieties and severe delusions, and had to be confined to a psychiatric hospital. After discharge she was placed on heavy psychoactive drugs. Robert mentions the fact that this is the first time that he has thought and talked about the possibility that there might be some connection between these experiences and his present inhibitions about sexual involvements.

Here we surely see Robert expressing a motivation for counselling and therapy that goes beyond the desire to "regain stability". He also indicates that he wants to talk about these frightening and disturbing experiences as a way of achieving contact with his own inner self. My impression is that he sees talking to me as a way of establishing a secure background, a firm footing from which he can stretch out his feelers towards a sphere that is both more difficult to penetrate and at the same time richer and more vital. In this first interview, however, these psychodynamic aspects are left unaddressed. Instead, we remain at a reality-orientated level of counselling—what Ellis (1980) calls "cognitive"—and concentrate on the inhibitions he has about exploiting his personal abilities and capacities as a way of instituting friendships and finding meaningful leisure-time activities. In our Socratic exchange, the patient realizes the irrationality of his conviction that a successful scholar must renounce all thoughts of a fulfilling private life. The patient is surprisingly gratified to hear the simple statement that free-time activities are necessary for a productive attitude to work. At the end of the first interview he imparts a relieved and more liberated impression.

In psychodynamic terms, it seems legitimate to explain the releasing effect of this first interview as a function of the way in which Robert projected on to his therapist the task of dealing with an unconscious inner dialogue between a strict, disciplining part of himself and an emotional, yearning part. As his counsellor or therapist, I assumed the task of "containing" these conflicts and working through them by means of inner visualization. For example, I was able to see the playful, emotionally needy young boy in my mind's eye, and to communicate with him at that level. In this I was not as restricted by a compulsive desire to control playful fantasies as the patient was.

> The second interview is again dominated by the controlled and collected attitude that Robert imposes on himself. He goes into more detail about the horror he felt at his girl-friend's psychosis. Then he reports a dream he has had between the first session and the present interview: "Outside, a fire is raging. I am sitting in a room with a friend, safe and sound. Outside everything is red, flames everywhere." The fireworks set off on New Year's Eve come to the patient's mind, and he comments that it is a time when anything can happen. Without telling him as much, it occurs to me that he experiences both his psychotic girl-friend and women in general as a menacing and fascinating "fire", and that he has withdrawn to the company of a therapeutic friend as a way of finding security. Of course, this is only a fantasy, but it characterizes my feelings in the further course of the session, in which Robert gives a relatively free account of his ideas,

preoccupations, and activities. In contrast to my psychodynamically orientated reflections, I keep the exchange with Robert to discussion of shared experiences, talking to him about a film he has just seen. He appears relieved. He seems to have latent fears that I am seeking to "pin him down" to a psychodynamic conflict.

Robert arrives at the third interview, fourteen days later, with the news that he has fallen in love. He has met a charming, attractive, intellectually stimulating woman student. He spends a lot of time with her and everything is just marvellous. In this session I sense that the considerable pressure and the self-imposed tension noticeable in the first two interviews have been dispelled. I also register the fact that Robert is withdrawing from me and is patently unwilling to enlarge on his new relationship with this young woman. This gives me food for thought. The idea that takes shape in my mind is that on the one hand Robert is making use of the security that I give him as an aid in approaching a woman. On the other hand, he does not want me interfering in the way he is accustomed to from his father. Once I have realized this, I let him take the lead with the choice of subject matter, and we talk about literary matters and his musical interests. After a short while, Robert changes the subject and tells me that he soon has to give a paper at the university. On the one hand he fears being laughed at if he makes a mess of his presentation, on the other he is afraid of arousing the others' jealousy if he does well. Recalling Beck's (1976) cognitive strategies, I encourage him to make use of his seminar paper to test his apprehensions for their rational justification. In addition, we go through an exposition *in sensu* simulation to the situation he fears, as suggested by behavioural therapists such as Emmelkamp (2004).

At our fourth encounter Robert speaks of commitment to a professional career, and indicates that he plans to embark on a steadier relationship with his girl-friend than he originally intended. He tells me that he has regained his ability to concentrate on his studies and sees exams as important opportunities for testing his own aptitude. But first he intends to take his girl-friend on a little trip to a town where he studied before coming here. The time he spent there was on the one hand carefree, on the other sometimes frighteningly lonely. He had lots of friends (of both sexes), they would eat together in the garden and talk. But there were also bouts of desperate solitude, despair at having no one for himself alone. Much as he wants to go on this trip, he is at the same time unsure whether it is a good idea. This strange lack of resolve, he tells me, is something he is only too familiar with.

I am reminded of his dream and say to him: "Perhaps you are afraid of being sidetracked or of losing your way altogether if—as in your dream—you look out of the window, go outside, and discover new avenues to explore." The patient responds: "I might go plunging down into the depths or find the door locked—fall into a deep hole, like I did six months ago."

A host of memories now come crowding back. Robert recalls how hard he found it to leave his parents when he went to see them for a weekend. On the one hand he feels he must not leave them alone, on the other he fears they might forget him if he goes his own way.

At the next session Robert tells me how well things are going for him. His paper at the seminar was impressive, and in his relationship with his girl-friend he feels freer than ever before in his life. By contrast, my impression of our exchange is one of triviality and boredom. Then it occurs to me that Robert may have needed me briefly as a bridgehead and is now ready to go his own way without me. I think to myself that, like every counsellor or therapist, I now have to face up to the difficulty of accepting my very limited significance for the patient. But I see the importance of gladness at the progress made by our patients, even if it comes about independently of our therapeutic interventions. Once I have thought this out, I realize that Robert is obviously not interested in carrying on with psychotherapy. In fact, Robert tells me as much, indicating in the further course of the hour that he now feels able to carry on without my assistance. He expresses his sincere gratitude for the benefit of an understanding encounter at short notice when he was going through a difficult period, and gladly accepts my offer that he can approach me again at any time if he feels the need for a psychotherapeutic exchange.

Crisis intervention

Anna is a post-graduate student working on her doctorate. She comes to a psychotherapeutic out-patients' department and expresses the fear that she will be diagnosed as a "psychiatric case" and confined to hospital because of her suicidal leanings. The psychologist conducting the initial interview sees her as highly inaccessible, trapped in a profound reactive–depressive crisis, and seriously in danger of committing suicide. However, in common with Anna, he ultimately judges her condition stable enough for her to keep her promise of not doing any harm to herself. On this basis he agrees to arrange an appointment with me for the following day.

In her exchanges with me, Anna is both physically and verbally extremely hesitant and slow-moving. Her gestures and facial expression are as if petrified. She herself says that inwardly she feels everything to be cold, hard, and rigid. Effortfully, and with many pauses, she tells me that the week before she parked her car in such a way as to cause an accident in which an old lady was injured. At this point, Anna clearly wishes to terminate the exchange, and her facial features relapse into their original immobility. Although inclined to go in search of further indications of major depression, I suddenly find myself surprised by a visual image. Prompted perhaps by some gesture or other non-verbal message, I suddenly have an image of a different side of Anna. I imagine her as a lively and attractive young woman. After losing myself in fantasies of this aspect of Anna for a few moments, although at the moment there is nothing apparent to connect her with them, I ask her, with a directness that I myself find surprising, about her longings, wishes, plans for her life. After initial hesitation, she tells me that a few weeks previously she had moved out of an apartment she had shared with a girl-friend for three years, and that this girl-friend was now living with Anna's former (male) lover. Anna had moved to a nearby town, at first in a mood of pleasurable anticipation. This mood had now evaporated. She tells me that she feels hopeless, and that her prospects for the future are bleak. This brings her back to the story of the accident. At this point, I once again have an involuntary visual image. I see Anna as a little girl, abandoned and unhappy. She has thrown away the doll she was playing with. As these fantasies take shape in my mind, Anna tells me that she would like nothing more than to dump everything, including her job at a university department. My impression is that, especially at the moment, this job is important to her, that it is significant and precious, like a toy in which she finds an expression of her own self. Accordingly, I go into her professional plans in great detail and am greatly struck by the commitment she displays to her work with the undergraduate students. Anna senses my interest. She becomes more mobile, outgoing. As she speaks of her personal disappointments, she thinks of her father's death. Again I have a vision of a little girl, this time running to sit on her father's lap after some disappointment or mishap. Anna tells me that she had a very affectionate relationship with her father until he was killed in a road accident five years previously. During her vivid account of all this—her gestures have now also become more lively—tears come to her eyes and she says she finds it humiliating to "break down and cry in front of someone else". She mentions her antipathy to psychotherapy, in which "everything the patient says is penalized with unmerciful understanding".

On the one hand I like the fighting spirit displayed in this criticism. But I am also aware of the stabilizing and supportive atmosphere that has developed during our encounter. Again I have the vision of the little girl who, for some reason, has been deeply disappointed by her mother and has thrown her doll into a corner in a temper. I ask Anna about her mother. She makes a wry face and says that all her life her mother believed she must sacrifice herself for others. She met her husband during the war and found running the home and bringing up the children anything but fulfilling. Her disillusionment communicated itself to her children. "You know all about that," she says, "a classical method, punishing children by depriving them of affection, that kind of thing." At this point I think of how unaffectionate Anna is in her dealings with herself, throwing herself away like an unloved, neglected doll-child. Apparently she sees it as my job to treat her and her doll better. I address the desire she has expressed to go as far away as possible from her present surroundings and get a job somewhere in North Germany. Anna's response is that she must escape the despondent effect her mother exerts on her. I have the impression that our exchange reaches a profounder level as Anna tells me that her mother has just been admitted to hospital for a bladder disorder (urethral ectopia). The patient's tone is clearly sceptical, and I ask her quite directly whether she fears her mother might have something malignant, possibly cancer. Anna responds with a timorous nod of the head; once again, tears come to her eyes. I say to her that it must be very difficult to confront her anger with her mother when her mother is so seriously ill. Thereupon, Anna becomes somewhat more animated and tells me that her relationship with her mother is ambivalent, more bad than good. Her successful older sister has much closer emotional ties with her mother, whereas her own feelings towards her are shot through with all kinds of resentment. She frequently has a terribly guilty conscience about this resentment and then wants nothing more dearly than to switch off everything inside her and bury it all for good.

Looking back over this first interview, I see how Anna has liberated herself from her profound depressive inertia and established contact with initially split-off parts of herself. She says that she now wants nothing more than to continue with her work as this is an important part of her life and also a source of support. She feels strengthened by my encouragement to pursue her leisure-time activities in the usual way.

> At the beginning of the next session (one week later), Anna is in a very reflective mood and affected by a marked degree of sorrow. She says that the end of her relationship with her boy-friend has obviously caused her a greater sense of loss than she cared to admit. She had seen her mother at the weekend and had a long talk with her that she keeps thinking about. She has also been dreaming "odd things". Pensively she gives me an account of individual dream fragments and the conversation with her mother. My impression is that Anna is increasingly able to develop integrated guilt feelings. As she imparts to me her insight that she cannot make unpleasant things simply go away by ignoring them, she makes an outgoing, attaching impression, and admits that she is glad to be able to come back to things talked over at the first crisis interview. She does not feel the need to embark on a more in-depth course of psychotherapy, preferring at the moment to concentrate on her work and her friendships. Feeling that she can now "get along" on her own, she says that she will consult me again if she ever needs any help.

A few weeks later, Anna calls me and says that she is very satisfied with her stability and the results of our crisis interviews. They had addressed things in her that she would like to engage with in the framework of extended psychotherapy. I give her the name of a colleague as I have no vacancies for long-term therapy at present.

Short-term dynamic psychotherapy

Roger (aged twenty-nine) consults me because of apprehension caused by ideas and visions that appear to him threatening and perverted. In addition, he has the impression that he "doesn't know who he is". Long-term therapy is out of the question, he says, as in four months' time he will be going abroad to complete an academic thesis. In the first interview, Roger appears on the one hand acute, outgoing, intellectually mobile, on the other hand despondent, out of sorts, overly well-adjusted, almost obsequious in his behaviour. Hesitantly he reports "funny" thoughts that he cannot get out of his head and the way they increasingly interfere with sustained intellectual effort. For example, seeing his girl-friend pass by outside, he suddenly imagines that she has amputated stumps instead of legs. He is alarmed by these visions, which also assail him when he is out jogging, for example, imagining that the jogger in front of him is having sodomist intercourse with a dog. In lectures he is frequently surprised by disturbing visions, such as that of a male member dropping out of the lecturer's mouth. As Roger tells me of these images that he finds peculiar and repulsive, the impression he makes on me is that of a sheepish, abandoned little boy who can (and will) only confide in a father figure who appears to him both benevolent and stable.

In contrast to these menacing visions, Roger is able to establish a friendly atmosphere during our exchange and despite the disgusting content of his fantasies I find myself taking a liking to him and an interest in his problem. I feel stimulated to entertain a number of thoughts and speculations and also to an emotional engagement of a kind a father might display towards a lively and gifted son. This latter is what suggests to me that a short-term course of psychotherapy is indicated. I later found the explanation for my positive transference. The father left the family when Roger was seven and since then has been treated by the mother as a criminal and the incarnation of evil. By splitting good and evil aspects of the father, Roger was in a position to initially shape the therapeutic relationship "from the positive side". The patient appeared to want to offset the splitting of good and bad subject and object representations by means of visual condensations, for example, the fantasy of the severed, threatening penis emerging from the mouth of his admired professor.

At our second session, Roger's profound loneliness becomes more apparent. He has to impose severe constraints on his inner liveliness, sexual activities like masturbation lead to tormenting feelings of guilt. In my counter-transference I experience a rather bored, indeterminate tension and think that, as Roger complains of being "kept at arm's length" by his girl-friend, a similar affective situation may have gradually established itself in his dealings with her as well. In the face of this suppressed liveliness, it strikes me that the patient lives very intensively in the visual images he describes as thronging in on him. I attempt to convey to him that his graphic and highly visual fantasies are both a possibility—and a capacity—for representing an inner situation of a disquieting character. Initially surprised at this, Roger then goes on to say that after the first interview he had already had the impression that I was able to relate to these "pictures" and this had taken some of the pressure off him. Back home, he had managed to regard these fantasies from a different perspective. In the course of the session, Roger recalls similar graphic visual images from his early childhood, experienced whenever he felt particularly lonely. He then goes on to suggest that this may have been his way of sustaining contact with the outside world. I confirm him in this, and put it to him that these visions may also have been a way of coming to terms with feelings of anger or annoyance. Roger appears to mull this over, then he recalls his suppressed annoyance and disappointment with his girl-friend. In fact though, he adds, he does not dare to perceive her in any other way than "right and true", because if he did that might mean the end of everything.

After this second interview, my impression is that my positive response to his visual imaginings and the appreciation of his fantasies as transitional objects have taken some of the superego pressure off Roger and at the same time afforded him a degree of narcissistic gratification. Subliminally, Roger appears to have experienced this as an alliance with an appreciative, drive-friendly, ancillary ego, an alliance that enables him to engage with his inner life and begin with the integration of split-off or rejected parts of his ego in which a great deal of vitality is pent up.

In the third hour, Roger reports that he is feeling rather relieved. He has recalled a childhood scene with his father. He has a graphic image of bathing naked with his father at the age of four. Though he must have seen his father's genitals, oddly enough they do not feature in the scene he sees before him, only a deep scar on his father's thigh. He then goes into a detailed account of his father, who for years had been completely expunged from his thoughts and memories. His father was a criminal and had often struck his mother. He served a number of prison sentences for robbery and housebreaking. After buying a car the family had selected together, he disappeared and Roger has never seen him since (he was seven at the time). Even before that, his father had been mixed up in obscure dealings abroad and frequently "vanished" for lengthy periods. I encourage Roger to go on a more probing inner quest for his father, and then it occurs to him that his mother had stylized him into the exact opposite of his father, a good, gentle boy as opposed to the evil, aggressive husband. At this point I put it to Roger that his fantasies may be a way of establishing relations with other aspects of his person-ality that he experiences as being aggressive. This sets him thinking about the scruples he feels at asking anything of his girl-friend and at accepting the sexual needs of his own body. The atmosphere of the interview changes; for the first time, he tells another person of his secret daydreams about his father: perhaps he did not come to a bad end in a criminal milieu, perhaps he went to America to become rich and famous. Roger finds himself frequently perusing the acronyms and initials of big American companies for indications of his father's name.

After this self-immersion in his fantasies and memories and discussion of things of immediate interest in his life, Roger tells me in the sixth hour that he has had a row with his girl-friend. He was so angry that he kicked his moped to pieces. I take him up on this and inquire after the moped, which is his means of transport to our interviews. Thereupon, he starts telling me of ideas about giving up his present way of life, going back to the factory where he used to work, and signing up as a casual labourer. The idea behind this is of "staying there forever and living with his mother" (the factory is located where his mother lives). In this back-and-forth between progressive (new job perspectives) and regressive (kicking his moped to bits, going back to mother) tendencies and the acceptance of his regressive urges, Roger starts engaging with his mother's problematic sides. He begins to ask himself what it was about her that made her take such a husband in the first place and then drive him out of the house.

We start the seventh hour by talking about Roger's self-damaging regression and withdrawal desires. Then he tells me he has taken up the saxophone again and got in touch with a former friend to arrange to make music together. After the last interview he had suddenly realized that there was absolutely no sense in sitting around at home waiting for affection. It was up to him to do something. On the other hand, he is worried by anxieties about his physical integrity and cleanliness. After a long evening with friends, he suddenly feared that there was something wrong with his digestion and that he might have got AIDS by drinking from the same bottle as the others. Both of us can understand how aggressive/expansive impulses endanger his pure, good, and gentle image of himself.

At this point, a substantial part of the short-term psychotherapy has already been achieved. Roger feels encouraged to engage with unpleasant internal and external perceptions. From the anxiety-free approach to impulses and thoughts taking shape within himself he derives energy to devote himself to his everyday life more uninhibitedly and flexibly.

In five further sessions, Roger engages with his ambivalent attachment to his mother. He senses the extent to which his activity confronts him with fears of losing the internalized mother, who is only willing to accept the good, round, tensionless child. Originally clouded by unconscious apprehensions, the prospect of the imminent period abroad takes on greater personal significance for his professional career and he is surprised to see the unalloyed pleasure his mother takes in his progress without the relations between the two breaking off. There are background doubts about whether his younger brother will oust him from his mother's internal life space.

At the end of therapy (in the thirteenth session), Roger tells me that at present the internal visions have become not so much frightening as interesting. He regards them almost as a treasure, particularly now that they have taken on a less fragmentary and destructive quality. He says that he is confident that things will go well, though he is rather saddened at the unavoidable termination of therapy and asks my permission to re-establish contact when he gets back from his stay abroad.

After this foray into the practicalities of counselling and psychotherapy, I shall now address the question of the basis of counselling and psychotherapeutic understanding. My approach to this is centred on modern hermeneutics. The first definition of hermeneutics is as a guide to the meaningful management of communal human existence. The focus then moves to aesthetic experience and the creative principles of counselling and psychotherapy. The concept of a *creative attitude* in counselling and psychotherapy is developed on the basis of these considerations.

CHAPTER FOUR

Hermeneutics: the art of creative understanding and life management

I n the view of its most prominent present-day representative, Hans Georg Gadamer, modern hermeneutics is no longer concerned exclusively with the interpretation of texts. Hermeneutic understanding is much broader in scope, a process in which, at a fundamental level, human beings understand, manage, and shape their individual and social realities.

All experience is conditional upon understanding. The human mind must be able to grasp the events crowding in on it if we are to experience ourselves as coherent individuals. In this sense, hermeneutic understanding is synonymous with the art of living. This art is one practised by each and every one of us in dealing with our everyday concerns, by teachers instructing their charges, by counsellors advising their clients, and by psychotherapists seeking to help their patients. It is invariably subjective, unique, it frequently defies reproduction, but for all that it does not stand in contradiction to rational thought.

Although, strictly speaking, the origin of the term hermeneutics has not been established beyond doubt, it is useful for our purposes to spend a little time looking at the role played by Hermes in Greek mythology. Hermes is first of all the herald and messenger of the gods, entrusted with the task of conveying, announcing, and translating divine messages to humanity. This makes him the interpreter not only of the laws from on high but also of Nature, which the Greeks understood as being divine. Hermes gives humans the language they need to experience and interact with the world. But also inherent in language is the possibility of concealment, distortion, and deception. It is in this context that we must regard the playful and roguish characteristics associated with Hermes.

The winged messenger Hermes accompanies the souls of mortals to the underworld, but he also assists mortals in this world, showing them the right way. With his staff he brings sleep to the restless, and his rod has the power to banish the Furies.

Despite his sometimes malicious jests, the beloved son of Zeus and the nymph Maia is described as loyal and as a bringer of good things. Hermes assists Zeus and Apollo in difficult situations. Despite the pranks Hermes often plays on him, Apollo holds the winged messenger dear as his "beloved brother."

The modern concept of hermeneutics derives from *hermenuo* "I designate my thoughts with words." In its broadest form, hermeneutics is both a theory and an art, the art of human understanding, above and beyond proclamation, explanation, and interpretation:

> Thus hermeneutics is more than a scientific method and much more than a designation of a certain group of scientific approaches. Above all, it refers to a natural human capacity. [Gadamer 1986, p. 301]

The understanding of understanding in antiquity is all-encompassing in the sense proposed by Gadamer. In the Middle Ages, this universality was split up and restricted to specific hermeneutic approaches—theological, philological, legal. The term "hermeneutics" itself was coined in the seventeenth century and the link with Hermes is controversial. Not until the modern age did this restrictive understanding of hermeneutics regain its initial amplitude and expand into a universal theory of understanding and interpretation. In Dilthey's work (1978), the psychological turn in hermeneutics then developed into a systematic recasting of the idea of *Geisteswissenschaften* (what we today usually call the "humanities") on the basis of psychological understanding. The concept of (subjective) experience (*Erleben*) is central to this new form of hermeneutics. A new expansion of the term to encompass all existence comes with Heidegger (1923). He sees the totality of human existence as "understanding", as "self-projection toward the possibility-of-self". Thus, understanding becomes much more than merely one of the "behaviours" of human thought. It is now the "basic movement of human existence".

Gadamer takes up where Greek philosophy left off and turns back to the reality of human living. Here, hermeneutics advances to a reflection of practical human life. In our context, it is essential to note the possibility of seeing everyday communication as one of the practical forms of everyday living. Gadamer himself describes hermeneutics as "the practical capacity for understanding as such, meaning the comprehending, empathic engagement with the other" (Gadamer, 1986, p. 301).

Thus, hermeneutics means not only the interpretation of texts but the understanding of others and ourselves. In this sense, it is a living process of interpretation carried out by the human subject in its own world (see cf. Ricoeur, 1965; Strenger, 1991). We shall now examine the foundations on which this assertion stands and inquire what form of understanding can indeed qualify as a living process of interpretation performed by human subjectivity.

Historicity and memory

The historicity of knowledge and experience is the first basic assumption on which hermeneutics rests. We are all caught up in a historical and social development that influences our feeling and thinking. Much—perhaps most—of what we understand is only properly understood when we have achieved adequate "historical" distance from it. This is as true of the events of human history as of the things that happen to us in our everyday lives. Freud used the term "deferred action" to express this insight. But the historical distance we require for understanding is only a special case of the experience of distance, of "standing back" from something. Gadamer speaks of the general hermeneutic function of "standing back" (*Abstand*):

> This distance is a hermeneutic principle active even in the case
> of simultaneity, for example in the encounter between persons
> seeking common ground in conversation. [Gadamer, 1986, p. 9]

In this view, otherness and distance is not a disruptive factor militating against the achievement of agreement or concurrence, but the very foundation that makes new experience possible in the first place. For human development (both individual and societal), the encounter with otherness is of essential significance. Just as contact with other cultures broadens our horizons, so we grow as individuals in our contact with others. Even the development of the mother–child dyad centres on the experience of otherness.

> Every such encounter makes us aware of something as a precon
> ceived opinion, something that was so self-evident to us that we
> were unable to realize the naïve equation with that which is truly
> our own, and hence the kind of misunderstanding that occurs in
> this way. [*ibid.*, p. 9]

It is this distance from (and to) others that acts as a corrective for our self-centredness and gives us something different to understand from what we initially assumed. In politics we observe the disastrous consequences of closing one's eyes to this insight. But at the individual level disregard of the experience of distance is equally harmful.

It may at first seem paradoxical that historical distance (including the distance to oneself) should be both formed and overcome by memory. What does this mean? Most counsellors and psychotherapists proceed on the realization that biographical experiences leave traces on our inner lives. Throughout our lives we are engaged in a "dialogue", sustained by moods and emotions, between ourselves and our parents, brothers and sisters, love partners, rivals, and many others. In conjunction with biological processes, the totality of these experiences defines our emotional and mental complexion and our behaviour. Psychological theory has coined an abundance of different concepts to refer to this everyday experience, which is familiar to almost all of us.

Psychoanalysis has been especially notable for its concern with the dynamics of past relationships with our fellows. It emphasizes the special significance of our first experiences with our mothers,

the perception of maternal affection or rejection, and the gratifica-
tions and disappointments that go with it. Persons with whom we
have relationships in our later lives and the experiences we share
with them also remain enshrined in our inner lives.

Freud has shown how damaging it is when clients and patients
succeed in fending off the presence of what they have been through,
the experiences undergone in their relationships, and the affects
bound up with them, because they appear too depressing, alarming, or shameful. The result of repression and splitting-off is not
only a loss of inner differentiation. Psychic and physical symptoms
indicate that these repressed or split-off parts of ourselves retain
their virulence. But even if clear mental or physical symptoms fail
to materialize, the price for the relief that the repression or splitting-
off of essential experiences may initially bring is high indeed: it
takes the form of feelings of futility, emptiness, diffuse moods,
disturbed selfhood.

In the case histories presented in the last chapter, we saw how
the patients were unable to bear certain aspects of their "internal
objects", by which I mean inner-psychic representations of significant others, and the feelings associated with them. They avoided
any kind of experience of distance and attempted to banish
unpleasant feelings and perceptions from their internal world. But
those feelings and perceptions retained their capacity for affecting
the patients' state of mind. As we saw there, awareness of difficult
situations and problems involving important reference persons is
not merely the detection of submerged facts. It is memory as the
appropriation of personal and interpersonal history.

For many clients and patients, it takes counselling and psychotherapy to enable them to gain possession of their personal history
and their life-world. Counselling and psychotherapy can be a stimulus for them to engage creatively with memories and assume the
authorship of their own lives. This model of memory as something
akin to a literary engagement with a subject is a necessary and
crucial complement to other models of the "way our minds work"
(physiological, neuronal, cybernetic, cognitive psychology). Its
concern is with the world of meaningful representations.

Memory and perception are tasks we are confronted with every
day. Normally, consistent subjective experience is a spontaneous
matter. Occasionally, however, it has to be wrested from the

ongoing march of events. The rebirth of the waking ego from the embrace of night that takes place every morning is described in masterly fashion by Marcel Proust:

> But for me it was enough if, in my own bed, my sleep was so heavy as completely to relax my consciousness; for then I lost all sense of the place in which I had gone to sleep, and when I awoke in the middle of the night not knowing where I was, I could not even be sure at first who I was; I had only the most rudimentary sense of existence, such as may lurk and flicker in the depths of an animal's consciousness; I was more destitute than the cave-dweller; but then the memory—not yet of the place in which I was, but of various other places where I had lived and might now very possibly be— would come like a rope let down from heaven to draw me up out of the abyss of not-being, from which I could never have escaped by myself. In one second I traversed centuries of civilization and from vague images of petroleum lamps and shirts with open collars my self reassembled itself anew in its original features. [1913–1927, pp. 5–6]

Here we have a suggestive literary proposal of how we might imagine the everyday re-emergence of our experience, our life-world, and our selves. When we assist our clients or patients in remembering their life-worlds, we are guiding them to what Gadamer would call the basic determination of human being. This understanding

> . . . is based on the fact that we have experiences of which we are aware. In the act of recall, these experiences take form as the understanding of meaning. [. . .] Such understanding of meaning is quite differently structured from the process of achieving new scientific knowledge. It is not a question of proceeding from one thing to the next and from there to the next again in order to derive a general truth by means of abstraction. The individual experience is of itself and invariably an entirety of meaning, a hanging-together. And yet its meaning relates to this entirety in a peculiar way. [Gadamer, 1986, pp. 31–32]

In a paradigmatic fashion, Freud illustrates this relatedness of the individual to the entirety of biographical experience with reference to dreams and neurotic symptoms. But even in our everyday experience, for example in erotic encounters, we sense the way in which we are permeated by the entirety of our personal history. And we know that subjective erotic experience would be destroyed if we took it out of its holistic context and made it exclusively the object of scientific research. The experience of art is probably very similar in this respect. Here again, we have no immediate knowledge of what it is that we experience so intensively. The profoundly felt encounter with a work of art places us in a hugely complex, differentially determined context of experience that affords us intense sensations. Once we step out of that context and scrutinize individual aspects in a way that divorces them from the emotional background of the experience, the intensity disappears.

Above and beyond intensity of subjective experience, the presence of historical experience enables us to achieve psychic continuity. Historical experience of this kind is only partially a conscious process of appropriation. To a large degree it is surely an acceptance of the fact that we are part and parcel of a historical setting that transcends us. If we can fully accept that, we will achieve what is normally referred to as a "rich" inner life. But we are not always able to fully accept things that happen to us and accept our own emotions for what they are. It is here that understanding psychotherapy intervenes. It helps its clients and patients to accept their subjective experiences with a view to filling the inner void that is left by the splitting-off of experiences. Seen thus, memory is a value in itself. In their radically "enlightening" approach, some schools of psychological thought make the mistake of regarding memories solely as a way of discovering circumscribed causes.

The omnipotence of historical enlightenment is mere semblance. It is precisely in that which resists this enlightenment and thus evidences its own duration of constant presence that the true nature of history lies. Myths [including personal myths; author's note] are not masks of historical reality that reason could lift off the true face of things. [. . .] The horizon of our historical awareness is not the myth-vacated, infinite desert of the enlightened consciousness. This enlightenment is rather historically conditioned and limited, a phase in the consummation of our destinies. It misunderstands itself if it thinks of itself as the un-destinied freedom of historical consciousness. But this means that history is what we were and are. It is the binding element of our destinies. [*ibid.*, p. 36]

Accordingly, when we help our clients or patients to a realization of their own histories, we are not merely revealing and uncovering, we are in fact completing their historical reality. I shall return later to this existential dimension of counselling and psychotherapy. It is more than the scientific examination of what a client or patient has learned on the cognitive plane, more than the uncovering of things repressed because of emotional conflicts. Naturally, these analyses are helpful in understanding historical reality, in the same way as standing back from the direct experience of a work of art—in a "rational" interpretation—can lead us to a more intensive experience of the work. The "plus" of historical experience in Gadamer's sense, over and against examinations conducted in a purely rational vein, depends crucially on the extent to which existential historical experience can be linked to language and representational structuring.

Language and narrative shaping

The language in which historical experience materializes is of a special kind. Unfortunately, language is frequently misunderstood in counselling and psychotherapy as a system of signs exclusively serving the communication of information. Then, statements made by clients or patients are treated like symptoms allowing conclusions about an underlying disorder or an acquired form of behaviour. This may indeed be an important factor in what clients and patients have to tell us, but it is never the "whole story". Effective language in counselling and psychotherapy has a value of its own—much like a novel that does not require academic interpretation in order to have an impact on us. We all know this from our own experience and the phenomenon is not difficult to explain. For language is not in the first instance a tool but rather an all-encompassing context of experience that we are born into.

> It is no more than a *façon de parler* when we say that acquiring language is a "learning" process. In fact it is a game, a play of imitation and exchange. Forming sounds and taking pleasure in those sounds is coupled with the first inklings of meaning in the imitative urge of the receptive child. No one can provide a sensible answer to

the question of when we first start understanding meaning. There has always been precedent pre-verbal apprehension of meaning, most prominently in the exchange of gaze and gesture, so that the whole process is in a state of flux [. . .] No one can genuinely grasp what it is that modern linguistics calls "language competence". [...] In fact, the term "competence" is only another way of saying that the language faculty taking shape in the speaker cannot be described as the application of rules and for that reason cannot be equated merely with the rule-governed use of language. We must regard it as the fruit of a free (within certain limits) process of linguistic practice when someone finally "knows" on the basis of his or her competence what is right and what is wrong. It is central to my own attempt to establish the hermeneutic principle of the universality of language in all understanding to regard learning to speak and the acquisition of orientation in the world as the indissoluble texture of the history of human education. [*ibid.*, pp. 5–6]

Learning to speak and orientation in the world—this close connection refers us to forms of counselling and psychotherapy that makes such existential speech possible. It is in this kind of speech that memory forms, memory and the consistent sense of individual selfhood. As I shall indicate shortly, I see speech, thus understood, as part of a larger phenomenon that I term narrative shaping. By this I mean that structured experience is formed not only through the things we are told and tell others, but also through an exchange with our own selves, through fantasies and thoughts, through the things we achieve in our objective, everyday world. Here too, individual persons find their way to an image of themselves and it is disastrous if they are deprived of such opportunities, say through unemployment.

But back to language. Language serves to make things not physically present visible in such a way that another can see them. And frequently the things I say will make another person see things I do not perceive myself. This is not necessarily an embarrassment. What I say can set off thoughts and fantasies that can broaden my own horizons when the other tells me of them. This fact is one of the reasons why the counselling and therapeutic exchange can be so effective.

As we have seen, in an extensive hermeneutic sense, language "in action" makes it possible to find our way round the world we live in. It is an inherited part of our lives, but, as Goethe put it so memorably, we will only truly possess what we have inherited if we actively acquire it.

> Rather, in all our knowledge of ourselves and in all knowledge of the world, we are always already encompassed by the language that is our own. We grow up, we gain familiarity with the world, and we become acquainted in the last analysis with ourselves when we learn to speak. Learning to speak [. . .] means acquiring a familiarity and acquaintance with the world itself and how it confronts us. [Gadamer, 1977, pp. 62–63]

Accordingly, the hermeneutic model of counselling and psychotherapy focuses on the establishment of a certain one-ness of experience. This makes it understandable that speaking of what has happened can serve the establishment of a coherent context of experience. In his essay "The universality of the hermeneutic problem" (1966, trans. 1977) Gadamer summarizes the point at issue.

> We are all acquainted with this, for instance, in the attempt to translate, in practical life or in literature or wherever; that is, we are familiar with the strange, uncomfortable, and tortuous feeling we have as long as we do not have the right word. When we have found the right expression (it need not always be one word), [. . .], then it "stands", then something has come to a "stand". Once again we have a halt in the midst of the rush of the foreign language, whose endless variation makes us lose our orientation. What I am describing is the mode of the whole human experience of the world. I call this experience hermeneutical. [Gadamer, 1976, p. 15]

The huge significance of the linguistic shaping of events that only become structured psychic experiences through symbolization is one that artists like the great novelists of the last century have confronted us with again and again. In his *A la Recherche du Temps Perdu*, Marcel Proust does not merely re-trace the past. He can only experience it as his own through linguistically structured memory. In *Ulysses*, James Joyce only establishes true contact with his own history and identity through the process of literary shaping. And Thomas Mann achieves a highly personal appropriation of his own existence—transformed into a mythic and world-historical dimension—in his *Joseph* tetralogy.

These documents of human intellectual endeavour are of relevance for counsellors and psychotherapists because they illustrate the significance of the "presentification" of subjective history/biography for psychic health. As narratives, they reveal a quasi-biological need for coherence. Rorty puts it as follows:

> We pragmatists think that the reason people try to make their beliefs coherent is not that they love the truth but because they cannot help doing so. Our minds can no more stand incoherence than our brains can stand whatever neuro-chemical imbalance is the physiological correlate of such incoherence. Just as our neural networks, presumably, are both constrained and in part constructed by something like algorithms used in parallel distributed processing of information by computer programmers, so our minds are constrained (and in part constructed) by the need to tie our beliefs and desires together into a reasonably perspicuous whole. That is why we cannot "will to believe"—believe what we like, regardless of what else we believe. [Rorty, 2001, p. 15]

In line with this, Gadamer sees coherent speech as the pivotal point of the human instantiation of meaning. But it is permissible to include pre-verbal communication and physical activity in the view of language as something that not only illuminates existence but makes it possible in the first place.

> Not only speech and writing, all human creations are invested with "meaning" that it is a hermeneutic task to read back out. It is this that substantiates the claim that all knowledge of the world is linguistically framed. [Gadamer, 1986, p. 198]

Gadamer, then, understands linguisticality in a superordinate sense. That means that the everyday products of human activity—the fruits of craftsmanship, a hobby, a friendly smile—are all encompassed by this definition. This is what enables us to draw upon a general model of narrative and representational shaping that sustains our existence. Here, I have my eye on the experience that memories and actions as such—even without interpretation—bring reality into existence.

In our context I see *representare* in its original sense of "letting something be present". This is not the same as a one-to-one relation to reality. The present experience will invariably contain representations of the past. This cannot always be conscious. The whole that is represented in the individual experience must remain latent, otherwise psychic and real acts would not be possible. Intrinsic both to action and language is a "completely unfathomable unconsciousness of itself" (Gadamer, 1960, p. 62). But what is it that distinguishes words, memories, ideas, and fantasies representing a rich fund of experience from the chatter, babble, and waffle that kills communication and leaves our inner lives void and vacant? When I turn to interactional experience later on, I shall attempt to give a more closely reasoned answer to the question. For the moment, it will suffice to establish that the characteristic feature of communicative experience is "that the objective not only becomes an image and idea, as in knowing, but an element in the life process itself" (Simmel, cited in Gadamer, 1960, p. 69).

Successful representation takes place when word and image co-generate the nature of whatever it is they seek to present. Thus in psychotherapy the work of memorialization will only succeed when it also opens up perspectives that go beyond the momentary. "Word and image are not mere imitative illustrations, but allow what they present to be for the first time fully what it is" (Gadamer, 1960, p. 143).

Gadamer refers to artworks as especially graphic instances of the function of representations in "instituting reality". In support of the conviction set out above that our simple everyday activities also fulfil the function of instituting reality, I should like to draw here upon the ideas of Susanne Langer on presentational symbolism. In *Philosophy in a New Key* (1942) she demonstrates convincingly that the pre-verbal symbolic material gradually collecting in an individual is a valid means of structuring inner experience. The material presented to the senses is already structured by the fundamental forms of perception. Even in small babies there emerges a presentational system that gives structure to the pandemonium of mere sensory impressions. These philosophical assumptions have been substantiated by research in developmental psychology (cf. Stern, 1985). Studies on mother–child interaction demonstrate the very early stage at which infants and small children structure their worlds by means of proto-symbolic modes of perception, ideas, and actions. Thus it is that, from the outset, human individuals compose their worlds.

The infant as artist? Indeed. At a later stage I shall discuss the way in which human individuals are caught up in a permanent creative exchange with the "materials" that come thronging in on them from their environment. Gadamer himself regards the artwork as the supreme form of the institution of reality to be found in all human activity. "The specific mode of the work of art's presence is the coming-to-presentation of being" (Gadamer, 1960, p. 159).

But this coming-to-presentation of being is more than the visualization of something that is already there. Rather, it takes this presentational shaping to create what is presented in a special way. Taking up Gadamer's thoughts and applying them to the everyday world, let us once more turn our attention to the infant. Research has shown beyond doubt that the nursling is already able to process the stimuli thronging in on it from within and without. With presentational symbols (sensations, auditory and visual experiences), it gives shape to what is initially devoid of form. It is in this way that the reality of the infant gains form. The same is true of the everyday dialogue between adults, to the extent that it goes beyond the communication of technical information. It, too, imposes a shape on experience. Thus, living dialogue and the inner shapings of experience that take place in everyday exchange (feelings, images generated by the mind, melody) all have a creative aspect that bestows a degree of consistency and continuity on the world of external occurrence. Hence my conviction that the everyday work of psychic and physical shaping, although of course less concentrated and less universal in its validity than a work of art, is deserving of the term "creative". This is also true of presentational symbols.

Although Gadamer has not made any explicit comment on this point, he does indicate the hermeneutic significance of non-verbal communication phenomena.

> The process of mutual understanding sets in at a more profound level of intersubjective communion and encompasses, for example, all forms in which consent comes about through silence [. . .] and equally the extra-verbal, mimic communication phenomena like laughter and crying, whose hermeneutic significance we have been taught to appreciate by H. Plessner. [Gadamer, 1986, p. 431]

Thus, the feelings, synaesthetic impressions, and as yet unshaped imaginings engendered in and by the psychotherapeutic situation, may indeed have a hermeneutic function, although they do not belong to the province of discursive thought. Like fully developed language, presentational forms of symbols serve the shaping of unintegrated events that would otherwise impair our psychological lives like foreign bodies (cf. Bion, 1962).

Interactional experience

Interactional experience is the third hermeneutic principle of counselling and psychotherapy. The concept of subjective experience (*Erleben*) was central to the psychological turn in Dilthey's hermeneutics (1900). In line with that theory, Gadamer derives the knowledge-forming function of experience initially from the dialogic nature of knowing. With historicity and representational shaping, the dialogic nature of knowing is a further basic principle of hermeneutics. The premise is that the objectivity and apparent absence of preconditions inherent in scientific discourse make it an inappropriate mode of gaining access to the individual and many-faceted form of experience represented by human encounter. According to Gadamer, continuity in the realm of the psyche can only be grasped in terms of life itself. Just as the individual notes of a melody only become what they are for that melody in the process of consummation, so in individual experience, as opposed to scientific experience, objective facts and events are not transmuted into general, abstract, discrete, and viable pieces of reality, but into factors in the life process itself. Thus, individual, personal experience always goes beyond all meaning that we believe we can know and hence possess. Lived life and lived experience are located in spheres formerly relegated to the realm of the aesthetic: sensations, impressions, sensory perceptions. "Aesthetic experience is not just one kind of experience among others, but represents the essence of experience per se" (Gadamer, 1960, p. 70).

It is this key status of sensory experience that prompts Gadamer to impose limits on the scope of validity of modern science. In his *Apologia for the Art of Healing*, he has this to say:

Modern science is not primarily knowledge of Nature as a self-balancing whole. It is not the experience of life that underlies it but the experience of doing, not the experience of equilibrium but of planned construction [. . .] The science that makes modern technological application possible does not understand itself as a filling of natural gaps and an incorporation into natural processes, but quite specifically as a form of knowledge in which the guiding principle is the reworking of nature to fit the human world, indeed the removal of the natural by virtue of rationally mastered construction. [Gadamer, 1966, p. 272]

Hermeneutics understands itself as a complement to the scientific experience and construction of our world. It enters into the field of tension between life-world and science and seeks to mediate between multi-faceted individual life experience and scientific statements that have congealed into anonymous signs. It attempts to discover meaning and significance in the subjective experience of the communal human situation. To follow Gadamer further, the discovery of a consistent and cohesive structure of experience that has not been atomized by science is in itself a communicative process. The "prior understanding" of the participants is employed in the process of understanding and, unlike firmly established prior knowledge that seeks simple empirical confirmation, it is kept fluid and susceptible of correction so as to achieve new perspectives. In search of understanding, the participants systematically bring their own preconditions into play.

The productive contribution of the interpreter belongs indissolubly to the meaning of understanding itself. This does not justify the private and arbitrary nature of subjective preconceptions. [Gadamer, 1986, p. 109]

Understanding is constituted in the understanding of the other. But where emotional elements are involved this is not a cognitive act, it is interactional experience. When someone understands what another says, this is not something merely stated, but something shared, something common to both" (*ibid.*, p. 19). This common experience is never complete. "Complete experience is not the completion of knowledge but complete openness for new experience" (*ibid.*, p. 271).

For Hegel (1807) the act of understanding is fully consummated in the understanding perception of the other. It is, thus, the construction of a shared truth and reality. Gadamer puts this as follows:

It is manifestly here that a central motive of all hermeneutics, the overcoming of other-ness and the appropriation of the other, achieves its specific, indeed unique form [. . .] To be in conversation means to be beyond oneself, to think with the other, and to return to oneself as another." [*ibid.*, p. 369]

For the encounter in counselling and psychotherapy, the change set off by this adoption of the other's perspective is relevant at both the cognitive and the emotional levels. It can also be regarded hermeneutically in terms of the constitutive coherence of part and whole. In the hermeneutic view, a single occurrence can be understood only in terms of an interactional whole. The understanding of an individual utterance reflects back on to that whole and gives it a new cogency. Thus, highly individual expressions of a human being—a literary text, a scenic form of interaction, or any other expressive manifestation of self—are related to the totality of the individual's personal life-projection, thus unfolding and changing the understanding of it.

In counselling and psychotherapy we speak of over-determination when a single scenic presentation, a dream, a free association, or a dialogic fragment encapsulates within itself almost everything that will only fully unfold in the process of counselling and psychotherapy. The special accentuation of the transference–counter-transference situation lies in the fact that systematic use is made of the affects surfacing in both participants and the graphic structuring of interactional experience. Thus, the hermeneutic situation in counselling and psychotherapy is not merely a communion of souls, as in the view of conversation found in Schleiermacher's Romantic form of hermeneutics (1819–1825). Effective hermeneutic understanding does involve the reception and acceptance of the other's emotional world in one's own experience, but it is reflected in—and reflected upon against—the background of personal life experience and established counselling and psychotherapeutic knowledge. In this way, the points of view encountered are changed and given a new form. This view of understanding as a "fusion of horizons" (Gadamer, 1960) and the emergence of common, shared meaning is a creative act placing hitherto unformed "material" within the active reach and scope of the subjects involved. In counselling and psychotherapeutic terminology we might refer to this as the integration of previously split-off or repressed experiences.

An ethical dimension of hermeneutics

As we have seen, hermeneutics regards itself as an essential complement to the scientific experience and construction of our world. For modern hermeneutics, its purview is the "text of the world", which we interpret and live out in our own individual ways. This makes hermeneutics a vital process of understanding and communication with one's own self. It is not a form of objectification. It does not seek a neutral stance with a view to establishing things beyond all reasonable doubt. The hermeneutically orientated approach involves not only the mind but also the heart and the spirit.

This experience, which articulates itself in corpo-reality and language, is bound to get in the way of the exactitude of the "exact sciences". That is why they have invented an artificial language of figures and formulas freed of all subjective experience.

The natural sciences progress constantly from the hitherto unknown to the now-known. Such a headlong development does not appear to be taking place in the sphere of interpersonal relations and self-knowledge. Humans are exposed to the same affects that they have always been called upon to curb, they pose the same questions now as they did 2,000 years ago, they are caught up in the same predicaments and concerns, the only difference being that the destructive potential of their technological ingenuity is now immeasurably greater than before. Hence, there is one major problem that refuses to go away: whenever we reflect on the application of science, the life-world and its ambiguous language returns to the centre of the stage. It has been pertinently remarked that, although science has developed rules for attaining knowledge, it has failed to develop any for the application of those rules.

In the subjective psychological sphere, we all remain enigmas to ourselves and others. It is from this undeniable observation that Gadamer derives the specific tension that informs human life. Self-identification in the course of personal development, human self-rediscovery and self-reinvention in each passing moment, is not mere poetic coincidence. It is the stuff of life and as such defies total comprehension by scientific means alone.

> It appears that the limitedness and finitude of life makes the conflict inevitable between natural science in its highest potential and human identity. It may be that here, beyond doing—that is, producing on the basis of a design—and controlling—that is, restoring balance and maintaining a direction under constantly changing conditions—a mode of behavior will gain significance that takes account of the limits imposed on the will to appropriation and that Aristotle consequently does not reckon to be inherent in *techné*: taking counsel with oneself, as practiced by the individual (or group) in situations calling for decisions. This is no longer the province of the specialist, who confronts others as one in the possession of the requisite knowledge. The knowledge required here is not supplied by science [. . .] What is required is counsel and consultation, which extends to an entirely different form of commonality than that represented by universal validity. It lets others have their say; it lets us have our say *vis-à-vis* others. Thus it cannot be ultimately and conclusively objectified in the style of a scientific proof, for it is more than the identification of the appropriate means to a well-defined end. Above all, it is an idea of what should be and what should not be, what is right and what is not. It is this that emerges, more implicitly than explicitly, as veritable commonality in counsel and consultation about what is to be done. At the end of such counsel stands not only the execution of a plan or the realization of a desired state, but a form of solidarity that unites all those involved. [Gadamer, 1986, pp. 168–169]

CHAPTER FIVE

Aesthetic experience and shaping of reality

The cases we described earlier demonstrate that the structured experience of the counsellor or therapist can help clients or patients to achieve a contour of experiential reality that makes symptoms superfluous as a way of structuring menacing occurrences. I shall now look more closely at the hermeneutic (language) game in counselling and psychotherapy and the way it encourages an enhanced aesthetic experience.

The significance of transitional objects for mental health

With a view to establishing the fundamental significance of the structuring process for mental health, I shall first describe my experiences with the so-called transitional objects proposed by the British paediatrician and psychoanalyst, Donald W. Winnicott. He proceeds from the everyday observation that for a small child some seemingly unremarkable object (a soft rag, a bit of blanket, a teddy bear) may have inestimable value. The child makes this object its own property and invests it with unique significance. This frequently only becomes apparent when the favourite comforter or the beloved teddy bear gets lost. The child is inconsolable and has lost something that cannot be replaced.

> But the term transitional objects, according to my suggestion, gives room for the process of becoming able to accept difference and similarity. I think there is a root of symbolism in time, a term that describes the infant's journey from the purely subjective to objectivity, and it seems to me that the transitional object (piece of blanket etc.) is what we see of this journey of progress towards experiencing. [Winnicott, 1971, p. 6]

Transitional objects are closely associated with the "transitional space" that is of fundamental importance for the child's growing self. The transitional space

> . . . is an intermediate area of experiencing, to which inner reality and external life both contribute. It is an area that is not challenged, because no claim is made on its behalf except that it shall exist as a resting-place for the individual engaged in the perpetual human task of keeping inner and outer space separate and yet interrelated. [*ibid.*, p. 2]

It is in this space that the infant's decisive experiences take place. Even the early maternal breast is not only objectively "there", it is subjectively experienced by the baby. The growing self of the child and its primary creativity is invariably invested in this experiencing process and what emerges is something else again: a transitional space with transitional objects. The acts of primitive creativity are, of course, fragile, and shot through with painful rejective states. But if the infant succeeds in internalizing the loving, giving, creative side of the mother, it will also gain the ability to invest a dead object with life and use it as a transitional object.

> Transitional objects and transitional phenomena belong to the realm of illusion which is at the basis of initiation of experience. This early stage in development is made possible by the mother's special capacity for making adaptations to the needs of her infant, thus allowing the infant the illusion that what the infant creates really exists. [*ibid.*, p. 14]

For adults, as for infants, the ability to create transitional objects and an intermediate area for personal subjective experience is of the utmost significance.

This intermediate area of experience, unchallenged in respect of belonging to internal or (shared) external reality, constitutes the greater part of the infant's experience, and throughout life is retaining in the intense experiencing that belongs to the arts and to religion and to imaginative living, and to creative scientific work. [*ibid.*, p. 14]

Winnicott's concept of transitional objects and phenomena is fascinating, and prompts a wide variety of interpretations. I focus here on the idea that a transitional object (a) represents the concretization of a relation between internal and external reality, and (b) is something that can be played with. In the process of mental maturation the child becomes increasingly independent of actual objects. In the bid to reconcile internal and external reality and achieve a certain "unity of experience", he/she plays with thoughts, ideas, and fantasies. But, as I shall show with reference to the hermeneutic function of aesthetic experience, this kind of play is in no sense contradictory to the attempt to come to terms with reality. Rather, it is an indispensable aspect of the human experience of reality. For the moment I wish to emphasize that in therapeutic interaction a verbal utterance, an idea, or a dream can all be regarded as transitional objects. As a pertinent metaphor, a fantasy, or a dream image, they can all mediate between objective and subjective reality and also between the conscious and the unconscious. In this way, the case histories demonstrated how objective events can be associated with subjective experience, thus engendering something that can serve as guidance and orientation.

But the area developing between counsellor and client, patient and therapist, an area in which words are formed and into which they are projected, also displays features of Winnicott's "transitional space". Once this common ground is established, and as long as it is not disrupted, we are "lost in a game" that Winnicott regards as absolutely vital.

It is assumed here that the task of reality-acceptance is never completed, that no human being is free from the strain of relating inner and outer reality, and the relief from this strain is provided by an intermediate area of experience which is not challenged (arts, religion, etc.). This intermediate area is in direct continuity with the area of the small child who is "lost" in play. [*ibid.*, p. 13]

In counselling and in psychotherapy, we repeatedly experience the way in which being "lost" in memories, images and fantasies is a structuring factor that asserts itself at certain junctures, for a longer or shorter period, and imposes a coherent shape on the internal reality of the patient and the way he or she perceives the world. It is in this sense that we must understand Winnicott's statement that a therapeutic relationship is productive when patient and therapist succeed in "playing with one another".

The idea of "playing games" has a banal connotation. To dispel this banality, I shall now discuss the existential significance of play. Reflection on the practical side of human existence reveals that play is of essential significance for consistency in our experience of the world around us and hence for our mental health.

Gadamer sums up two thousand years of philosophical thinking when he describes "playful behaviour" as one of the foundations of successful understanding and hence ultimately of successful living. Play fulfils a meaningful and salutary function.

> In playing, all those purposive relations that determine active and caring existence have not simply disappeared, but are curiously suspended. Playing takes place not only "for the sake of recreation" but also serves to remedy detrimental impulses and moods. [Gadamer, 1960, p. 102]

Gadamer provides a detailed rationale for the effectiveness of the psychotherapeutic language game. Like Winnicott, he derives adults' language games from the spontaneous employment of sounds and gestures in children's games and the response of their immediate environment to this activity. Accordingly, it is natural for us "to think of the universally linguistic nature of our experience of the world in terms of the model of a game" (Gadamer, 1986, p. 5).

In counselling and psychotherapy, as in children's games, adult speech, and artistic activity, we find ourselves confronted with an area of play related contrapuntally to everyday life. Here, too, memories, ideas, and notions are "played with" in a way that transcends immediately purposive activity. Like artistic activity in the narrower sense of the term, therapeutic language games serve both the development of our patients and a constructive approach to internal and external reality. What forms do these language games take?

First of all, I shall draw upon Wittgenstein's concept of the language game (1953) to substantiate the truth-content of psycho-therapeutic interaction. In his long and passionate engagement with the problem of determining the truth-content of a language utterance, he finally came to the conclusion in his late work that it is only in the speech act itself that we can establish whether an utterance is true. This truth is not objectifiable, it can only be determined in terms of whether or not the utterance is beneficial to the given communicative situation. That means that an utterance is true if the person it is addressed to can use it to continue his language game. In all forms of psychotherapy based on understanding, this criterion of "communicative utility" takes on a crucial significance; for example, in Sullivan's consensual validation (1953). This has always been of major importance for psychoanalytic forms of therapy (cf. Schafer, 1983). On the role of language games in constructing truth, Gadamer has this to say:

> Language games exist where we, as learners—and we do we cease to be that?—rise to the understanding of the world. Here it is worth recalling what we said about the nature of play, namely that the player's actions should not be considered subjective actions, since it is, rather, the game itself that plays, for it draws the players into itself and thus itself becomes the actual subjectum of the playing. The analogue in the present case is neither playing with language nor with the contents of the experience of the world or of tradition that speak to us, but the play of language itself, which addresses us, proposes and withdraws, asks and fulfillss itself in the answer. [Gadamer, 1960, p. 490]

In counselling and psychotherapy, this "understanding of the world" takes place between two or more persons. Winnicott says:

> Psychotherapy takes place in the overlap of two areas of playing, that of the patient and that of the therapist. Psychotherapy has to do with two people playing together. The corollary of this is that where playing is not possible then the work done by the therapist is directed towards bringing the patient from a state of not being able to play into a state of being able to play. [ibid., 1971, p. 38]

Caper (1996) and Parsons (1999) regard the playful distance taken up vis-à-vis reality (such as we find in humour) as essential for successful psychodynamic understanding. A successful language game means that a person stands in structured linguistic or presentationally symbolic contact with his/her own internal and external reality. This is relatively easy to discern in concrete therapeutic situations. Whether or not a patient hears the linguistic intervention of the therapist, builds on it to generate new ideas and memories, and gradually frees himself of anxieties and symptoms by way of this enlargement of his psychic perceptiveness, is a process that can be established empirically.

Freud is much more critical of the role of play in coping with reality. By virtue of its origins in "hallucinatory wish fulfilment" and the "omnipotence of thoughts", play and fantasizing helps to evade the pressure of critical reason. The person indulging in fantasies, dreams, and games behaves autoerotically or narcissistically.

> Nevertheless the mild narcosis induced in us by art can do no more than bring about a transient withdrawal from the pressure of vital needs, and it is not strong enough to make us forget real misery. [Freud, 1926, p. 81]

On the other hand, Freud also emphasizes that play does not exclusively serve the pleasure principle but can also help to cope with reality:

> In the case of children's play we seemed to see that children repeat unpleasant experiences for the additional reason that they can master a powerful impression far more thoroughly by being active than they could by merely experiencing it passively. [Freud, 1920, p. 35]

Thus, the function that infantile play, adult fantasies, and artistic activity have in common is that of bringing together the reality principle and the pleasure principle. The negative side of creative play with ideas and artistic activity is, on the one hand, neurotic immersion in daydreams that have no contact with reality and, on the other, trivial aestheticism. In contrast to these neurotic variants, successful play, the activity of imagination in children and adults alike, finds its way back into a reality enriched by new perspectives.

Creative writers have repeatedly indicated how the ego is formed through play. But they have also confronted us with the way in which this play is shot through with cruel failures that have thrown more than one of them completely off course. Even undisputed geniuses are caught up in a constant struggle between playful intuition and crippling toil—which all serves to confirm Goethe's dictum: genius is hard work.

Aesthetic structuring in counselling and psychotherapy

Memories, ideas, and fantasies surfacing in counselling and psychotherapy can be regarded as aesthetic experiences. There is a frequent tendency to ignore an insight that aesthetic theories from Baumgarten (1741), Kant (1799), and Hegel (1812) to Dewey (1934), Langer (1942), and Adorno (1970) consider to be axiomatic: central psychological concepts like sensation, imagination, and subjective experience are aesthetic categories. For this reason alone, I intend to discuss the role of aesthetic experience in counselling and psychotherapy in greater depth. With recourse to aesthetic theory we shall see more clearly the precise value that sensorially experiential remembered images, scenic visions, and fantasies have for our self-knowledge, and the way they structure the therapeutic setting and the internal reality of clients and patients.

The ancient Greek term *aisthesis* refers to the theory of sensory perception, imagination, and sensation. In Greek philosophy, these forms of human experience are allotted a special function in the knowledge we have of our life-world. In the Middle Ages, purely intellectual knowledge (*gnoseologica superiora*) was placed on a higher plane than sensory or aesthetic knowledge (*gnoseologica inferiora*). Not until the modern age did Baumgarten, the champion of a new philosophical form of aesthetics, re-establish aesthetic knowledge as central to our "representation of the world". Of interest to counsellors and psychotherapists is the way in which central concepts like "memory" and "subjective experience" are seen as fundamentally aesthetic (as opposed to logical) categories serving the establishment of knowledge. Baumgarten speaks of "esthetic empiricism" and "the art of esthetic experience through which we are empowered to feel things clearly" (1741, p. XVII).

Despite Baumgarten's efforts, the philosophy of the modern age favoured a restriction of the concept of aesthetics to questions of taste and art. By contrast, Gadamer's hermeneutic approach, from which the present study takes its bearings, squarely re-establishes aesthetic experience as a central factor in the understanding process. All practising counsellors and psychotherapists will have clients and patients who are extremely adept intellectually. Yet they may still feel disorientated to a point of despair that leads them to contemplate suicide. They are unable to use their faculty of thought as an instrument for giving their existence meaning and structure. They are exponents of that crisis of modernism that produces a yawning gap between the experience of our life-world and the scientific grasp of our world. As we have seen, the hermeneutic approach sets out to open up an aesthetic and practical dimension of experience that can pave the way to a consistent experience of the world. But the various forms of aesthetic escapism with which we are confronted today makes it necessary to stress the fact that we are appealing to aesthetic practice here as a way of understanding real life.

Inspired by Gadamer, the literary studies expert Jauss (1982) explicitly elevates the three basic aesthetic functions *poiesis*, *aisthesis*, and *catharsis* (the productive, receptive, and communicative sides of aesthetic experience) to the status of key elements in the meaningful experience of reality.

Poiesis designates the productive side of aesthetic experience. "And as the ordinary mortal falls silent in his torment, a god gave me the power to say what I suffer" (Goethe, 1981, 'Trilogy of Desires'). What this means is not merely discharge and relief but a structuring process in the service of the integration of experience. Underlying *poiesis* is a general need to feel at home in the world and in one's own self. As I have shown with reference to Gadamer, the active shaping of words or images tempers the alien nature of the internal and external world.

> The full profundity of esthetic experience is not achieved by the keen perception of the new or surprising difference of an unknown world. It is rather the gateway these things open up for the recognition of submerged subjective experience, for the retrieval of time we believed had gone for ever. [Jauss, 1982, p. 43]

For a clearer understanding of the receptive side of aesthetic experience, let us recall the original meaning of *aisthesis*—understanding by seeing.

Aisthesis as the basic receptive esthetic experience thus accords with various definitions . . . that understand the enjoyment of the esthetic object as an enhanced, deconceptualized, . . . renewed vision, . . . in short "complex perceptual acuity" and thus rehabilitate the acquisition of knowledge through the senses over and against the primacy of knowledge through concepts. [*ibid.*, p. 43]

The third element in aesthetic experience, *catharsis*, is widely understood (e.g. by Freud) in Aristotle's sense of the term as an emotional discharge:

He who witnesses a performance can be affected by it, identify with the protagonists, give free rein to the passions thus excited, and experience pleasurable relief in their discharge, as if he had been subject to a healing process. [*ibid.*, p. 73]

But we must note that this conventional interpretation of *catharsis* is a foreshortened one. It takes insufficient note of the communicative function. Catharsis refers to *shared* affective experience. As a form of experience induced in one individual by another, it serves both the practical exploitation of aesthetic experience for the communication of views and modes of experience and the stimulation of practical action. In this sense, aesthetic experience opens out into dimensions that have relevance for the practical conduct of our lives.

For some counsellors and psychotherapists, placing the emphasis on the aesthetic factor may appear too "hands-off", despite the links we have indicated between aesthetics and practical activity guided by the senses. But hermeneutically orientated counselling and psychotherapy will indeed do all it can to avoid an "intervention" in the psychosocial links that are part and parcel of a client's or patient's life. The decision about what to do and what not to do is left entirely to the clients and patients, once they have become aware of the conflicts conditioning their lives. This appears to me to be an important point in connection with the ethical issues involved in psychotherapy. For an excellent review of this aspect, the reader is referred to the work of Otto Dörr Zegers (1996).

The significance of the three basic aesthetic functions for counselling and psychotherapy can be specified more accurately with reference to the psychoanalytic concept of projective identification. Initially, unstructured experience takes shape in words, images, and feelings. The form thus imposed upon it is communicated to another person, frequently in a fragmentary, pre-conscious way. It seems legitimate to regard this as a form of projection, without necessarily allotting a pathological function to it. The therapist receives the message and incorporates it into the *ambiente* of his own experience. This reception is a structuring process because the therapist represents within himself the patient's history and life-world and assembles a complex picture of the patient in his own mind. The patient relates to this internal image formed by the therapist—a product of receptive aesthetic perception—by means of verbal and non-verbal messages. In the ideal case, he will perceive and recall aspects of himself hitherto concealed from him, achieve a more graphic and better-structured active engagement with his conflicts, and attain a more holistic subjective experience of himself with the aid of the counsellor's or therapist's emotional cathexis. This communicative side of counselling and psychotherapy expresses itself in a fuller perception of self and demands to be seen as a fundamentally aesthetic experience.

Aesthetic perception and truth

When we develop the feeling that both everyday and artistic structuring helps us not merely to experience the world but also enhances our knowledge of it, then this conviction is initially a subjective one. For Gadamer, it is art more than anything else that conditions our senses for genuine living. Unlike scientific information, artistic experience is never unequivocal. He illustrates the point with reference to Velazquez' *Las Meninas*.

> A courtly scene, but at the same time a self-portrait of the painter. Of the picture taking shape we see only the rear side of the canvas. This picture within a picture excites a curiosity in the beholder that goes beyond the figures in the foreground, the princess, her lady-in-waiting, the dwarves. The painter's gaze also takes us beyond them. Perhaps he is painting a portrait of the royal couple only visible in the mirror at the back? There is no way the beholder outside the picture can decide. But there is another beholder, a beholder *within* the picture, the man in the open door at the rear. He is gazing at the picture within the picture but he cannot tell us what he sees.

Every detail of the picture is clear—but the picture as a whole remains an enigma. Velazquez has not merely painted a picture of courtly life. His real subject is the mystery of art. And this is also the subject of hermeneutics. For the hermeneutic view, the truth of a work of art is indefinable. It lives only in the history of the interpretations the work inspires. And also where art responds to art. Picasso, for example, interprets Velazquez by taking up where he left off, painting his picture anew. The history of artistic impact is also this dialogue conducted by artists and their works over the centuries. [Gadamer, 1996, pp. 10–11]

In an interpersonal encounter we also immerse ourselves in a history of this kind. Even in our everyday exchanges, as soon as we grant ourselves and others the freedom of thought, we sometimes arrive at a point where we have never been before. New perspectives form in a process of what Gadamer calls a "merging of horizons". The truth of a counselling or therapeutic interview cannot be defined beforehand. It battens on the authenticity and uniqueness of the communication between patient and therapist. By its very nature, the authorship of his or her own life aspired to by the patient cannot be explained by any scientific method.

The aesthetic aspect of counselling and psychotherapy confronts us with relativity and evanescence. Those anxious for scientific "certainty" are likely to fear the bugbear of arbitrariness. But history itself makes us both transitory and continuous. This is an *aporia* inherent in existence itself that we should not deny concretistically, but make use of as a stimulus for personal creativity. Gadamer sees this incorporation into transitoriness and duration, passivity and activity, receptiveness and creativity, expressed cogently in a poem by Rainer Maria Rilke with which he prefaces his magnum opus *Truth and Method*.

> Catch only what you've thrown yourself,
> all is mere skill and little gain;
> but when you're suddenly
> the catcher of a ball
> thrown by an eternal partner
> with accurate and measured swing
> towards you, to your centre,
> in an arch
> from the great bridgebuilding of God:

why catching then becomes a power —
not yours, a world's.

He who catches "what he has thrown himself", who plays with his own thoughts, images, insights, and ideas, is the gifted one who remains ultimately reproductive. The catcher of the ball "from the great bridgebuilding of God", he who has genuine insight into the cosmic, the timeless, the transcendent, and is gripped by it will not remain caught up in himself but will be receptive for the meaning of "a world". He is not a creator but a recipient, just as fulfilled human experience and great art takes shape when it can receive and create the species of truth that transcends both the individual and history.

The aesthetic dimension of everyday experience

In *Art as Experience* (1934), the American philosopher John Dewey examines the way in which we gain knowledge of our life-world through the senses. He deplores the fact that this kind of experience and its reflection in aesthetic theory is divorced from the everyday practicalities of our lives and relegated to a special area, that of art.

> The hostility to the association of fine art with normal processes of living is a pathetic, even tragic, commentary on life as it is ordinarily lived. [Dewey, 1934, p. 34]

The very first cave paintings demonstrate that human activity invariably has both a purposive aim and an aesthetic dimension. The modern dissociation of ordinary experience and aesthetic experience has negative repercussions on the way we handle our lives by underrating the sensuous quality of everyday experience and neglecting its potential as a source of the joy we take in life. Like artistic experience, everyday experience is distinguished by its uniqueness, its sensuous immediacy, and its holistic nature. Thus, Dewey urges, we must restore the "continuity between aesthetic experience and the ordinary processes of living". He sees this as crucially important for our psychic health because it enables us to give coherence and meaning to the constant stimulation of the senses bearing in on us.

Anthropologically, aesthetic experience needs to be seen in connection with primitive rituals.

Only those who are so far removed from earlier experiences as to miss their sense will conclude that rites and ceremonies were merely technical devices for securing rain, sons, crops, success in battle. Of course they had this magical intent, but they were enduringly enacted, we may be sure, in spite of all practical failures, because they were immediate enhancements of the experience of living. Myths were something other than intellectualistic essays of primitive man in science. Uneasiness before any unfamiliar fact doubtless played its part. But delight in the story, in the growth and rendition of a good yarn played its dominant part then as it does in the growth of popular mythologies today. Not only does the direct sense element—and emotion in a mode of sense—tend to absorb all ideational matter but, apart from special discipline enforced by physical apparatus, it subdues and digests all that is merely intellectual. [Dewey, 1934, pp. 36–37]

Dewey's view leads us to the conclusion that aesthetic experience is a guide in human living and especially in our knowledge of good and evil. Accordingly, sensuous experience, distinguished as it is by immediacy, unity, and emotionality, takes on a special moral function.

The dispute about the ethical and moral significance of aesthetic experience is very old. Plato saw sensuous experience and art as a source of deception. He saw ideas cleansed of the sensory element as bearers of a higher truth. Since then, there have been adherents both of this view and of its opposite, sensing appalling dangers in the divorce of our own selves from immediate sensuous experience, as in modern science and technology (e.g. Horkheimer & Adorno, 1944).

A case in point is the dispute about the Jewish poet Paul Celan (see Felstiner, 1995). In his famous *Death Fugue*, Celan gives a sensuous and aesthetic portrayal of the reality of the Holocaust. Many of his readers, including the present writer, feel that such an approach to the issue is emotionally more immediate, and hence ultimately more meaningfully truthful, than abstract facts and figures. Jorge Semprun, who in *Literature or Life* (1997) describes his incarceration in the Buchenwald concentration camp, is another author who appeals to art as the chief witness of subjective and objective reality:

> Not that what I experienced was unsayable. It was unbearable, but that is something else, as will be readily understood. Something else that has nothing to do with the form of a possible account, but with its substance. . . . Only those will find access to that substance . . . who contrive to transform their testimony into a work of art, a space of creation. . . . But that is nothing unusual. It is the same with all major historical experiences.

The view is also taken by Gilbert J. Rose in his book *Necessary Illusion—Art as Witness* (1996). For him, art reveals a reality that would otherwise be hidden from us. Elias Canetti puts it this way:

> We have no knowledge of what we feel; we have to see it in others in order to recognize it. What we recognize only becomes real after we have experienced it beforehand. It first lies within, without our being able to name it; and then, all of a sudden, there it is, as a work of art, and what happens to others becomes a memory within: at this moment it becomes real. [quoted by Rose, 1996, p. iix]

Now that we have described the hermeneutic and aesthetic foundations of human living and in this process have repeatedly encountered the idea of a creative attitude in counselling and therapy, it is time to attempt a cogent description of this attitude in more universal terms. This is the subject of the next chapter.

CHAPTER SIX

Creative principles of psychotherapy

I n the following I shall be taking aspects of the hermeneutic and aesthetic theories outlined above and applying them to the case histories discussed in Chapter Three with a view to deriving creative principles effective in psychotherapy.

Historicity and memory

As we saw in Chapter Three, persons receiving counselling or undergoing short-term therapy are able to engage with threatening thoughts and ideas within the protective framework of a therapeutic relationship. The patient who came for psychotherapeutic counselling (Robert) describes his life-situation first of all in terms of a development that appears to be heading for a crisis. The image that takes shape in the mind of the counsellor is that of the patient's interaction with his own self: "Doctor with an acute clinical view of things who critically scrutinizes the disclosures made to him." This image taking shape in the therapist's mind puts the patient in touch with one aspect of his relationship with himself. It gives him a heightened perception of himself and the therapeutic situation affords him the necessary hermeneutic distance ("standing back") to establish contact with an aspect of himself that was previously inaccessible to him. This represents the onset of the hermeneutic "overcoming of othernesss" on the part of the patient.

A similar process is observable in the crisis-intervention patient (Anna). She too initially has no access to central areas of her inner world. The therapeutic exchange enables the patient to perceive essential aspects of her inner and outer world, which then lose their distressingly alien character.

In the example of dynamic short-term therapy (Roger) we also witness a process of appropriation of psychic reality. Through memory and inner-psychic perception the patient is able to overcome his alienation from himself and his experiences.

The differences between the three procedures described— psychotherapeutic counselling, crisis intervention, short-term psychotherapy—consist in the scope of the perception and memory work involved. While in the counselling example the patient was able, with the help of the therapist, to clarify a situation causing him immediate distress, the crisis-intervention patient was able to recognize and localize a "central relation-conflict issue" (Luborsky *et al.*, 1988) and the way it was conditioned by aspects of her own personal biography. The patient undergoing short-term psychotherapy went even further in this respect, finding his way to a more integrated self through the perception of longings that dated back to a much earlier stage in his development. This rendered the psychic symptoms superfluous that ("in the face of an alien process that causes us to lose our bearings") had served to structure diffuse and ill-defined feelings.

Language and narrative shaping

In all three cases, the shaping of experiences via representations in the form of imagination and verbalization are of fundamental significance for the course of counselling and therapy. These representations first of all give expression to experiences that have hitherto not "materialized" as such. In so doing they provide the therapist with more than the information he/she needs to draw logical conclusions. More importantly, the hermeneutic exchange enables the patients to discover covert aspects of their own selves. It appears that the graphic apprehension of these aspects is the more significant part of the discovery process than the logical conclusions about underlying conflicts. These sensory apprehensions and imaginings represent hitherto unshaped events of a distressing nature. Through these aesthetic representations the patients become more integrated and structured.

Creative shaping within the psychotherapeutic language game enables the patients to find a support (something to "hold on to") in the diffuse and ill-defined process threatening them. For the person speaking, verbal and presentational symbolic shaping allows him/her to apprehend something not initially visible. In this process, dismaying and depressing experiences lose their dulling and inhibiting impact. In Robert's case we see how psychotherapeutic counselling helps him to apprehend and shape his helpless despair and confusion in the face of an abortive relationship and the separation from his parents. The patient succeeds in apprehending the "helping relationship" with the therapist in the form of a dream. Although this dream is surely of major significance in structuring psychic experience, it is left uninterpreted. Yet as an aesthetic materialization it appears to mean something to the patient and has a salutary effect even without interpretation.

The crisis-intervention patient, Anna, succeeds not only in talking about her experiences but in achieving a graphic apprehension of what initially weighed on her like an amorphous burden. In her mind's eye she visualizes her mortally sick mother and vividly pictures the disappointment pent up inside her and the profound resentment she feels *vis-à-vis* her mother.

The short-term psychotherapy takes a similar course. In the psychotherapeutic language game Roger's longing for his (a) father takes tangible shape instead of remaining in the unintegrated form of a symptom. Through aesthetic shaping in the form of apprehension and imagination, this longing no longer needs to be split off but can be integrated into the patient's psychic *ambiente* in the form of an image. This enables him to re-engage in the dialogic encounter with himself and subsequently he also succeeds in re-establishing a dialogue with his real reference persons.

Interactional experience

The third hermeneutic principle informing creative psychotherapy is "interactional experience." I have already emphasized that the crucial factor in hermeneutic exchange lies in the opening up of new perception horizons. This is largely effected by the therapist sympathetically accompanying the patient into his/her internal and external world. My graphic and scenic understanding of this process is that the therapist allows himself/herself to be taken into the patient's world and shares the experience not only of the patient's own feelings but also those of persons closely involved with the patient. The important thing is that this shared experience should be given a narrative shape so as to avoid getting bogged down in vague and ill-defined feelings. The therapist's sympathetic interest alone (independently of interpretation) can encourage the patient to perceive things of an unpleasant and shameful nature and embark on the work of narrative shaping.

Accordingly, patients do not merely give the therapist information so that he or she can draw (psycho)logically correct conclusions from it. Of greater moment is that the patients should invite their therapists to go along with them into their life-world and engage in a scenically shaped interaction game. Robert, the young man who came for psychotherapeutic counselling, evokes in the therapist the image of a patient who observes himself from the vantage of a doctor with an acute clinical view. The therapist would himself be intimidated and experience great fear of shame if he were constantly exposed to such a gaze. On the basis of his inner scenic actualization he is able to understand his patient's fear of a love relationship.

The crisis-intervention patient, Anna, evokes in the therapist the image of a lonely little girl who has thrown away her doll in a fit of temper. He then knows how important it is for there to be a person who can help the little girl to reaccept her doll as the representation of her relationship to herself.

Roger, the patient undergoing short-term psychotherapy, quickly reverts in the psychotherapeutic situation to the status of a little boy in search of his frightening but longed-for father. By displaying his interest in this little boy, the therapist indicates that it is also important for the patient to engage with this aspect of himself.

I believe I have demonstrated that scenic representations are the medium through which both the therapist and the patient make their way into an inner (hi)story. The therapist sees the dismay of the young man in the face of his psychotic girl-friend, he sees the rage of the young man after the injuries she has experienced, he sees the fears of the patient forced to go his own way without a paternal companion to give him the security he needs. The crucial element in hermeneutically inspired psychotherapy is that the therapist should engage emotionally with the things apprehended in a scenic form. As the case descriptions illustrate, the therapist remains at the scenic level of the patient's language game. Within this shared experiential space, he puts the patient in contact with his/her scenically shaped experience. The patient can then decide whether the therapist's apprehensions expand his/her own perceptions and can be drawn upon for the shaping of his/her experience.

With Robert (psychotherapeutic counselling) this process remains at a rudimentary stage. The patient evokes in the therapist the feeling that he would like the support of a paternal friend in weathering the turbulences experienced with his female partners. As a psychoanalyst, I would assume the presence of a fended-off oedipal conflict with latent homosexual and oedipal leanings towards a person representing the father. In hermeneutic counselling such constellations may be perceived but they cannot be worked through. The important thing is that the therapist co-experiences in a scenic form the anxieties of the patient and also his need for a stabilizing partner. Then the therapist will be able to assume the role of such a partner, give him the security he is looking for, and help him to fulfil this function for himself. In the crisis intervention and short-term therapy examples the situation is similar. Here again it is less a matter of interpreting what has occurred than of helping the patients to admit split-off parts of themselves into their own experience through the agency of the therapist's own structured experience.

Summing up, we can say that perception, narrative shaping, and interactional experience can integrate "undigested" experience into the patients' psychic *ambiente* and thus make them into significant experiences. This offsets their alienation from the events in question and their own selves, and enables them to achieve coherent subjective experience.

A creative approach, taking due account of the hermeneutic principles described above, can serve as a feasible basis for counselling and psychotherapy. In individual cases, these principles can be supplemented by various psychotherapeutic techniques. The elements of such a creative approach can be derived from the three hermeneutic principles we have discussed. The principle of historicity and memory is a central factor in the cultivation of "competent empathy" for the internal and social reality of clients and patients. The principle of the linguistic nature of understanding is instrumental in "creative imagination" in connection with psychic and social reality, while the principle of subjective experience is closely associated with the cultivation of "interactional perception". I shall now examine these essentials of a creative, hermeneutic approach separately.

Competent empathy

The clients and patients described in our case histories were enabled, by the treatment they were given, to establish contact with significant internal modes of experience and also with external aspects of their life-worlds. The patient who underwent psychotherapeutic counselling was able to perceive the experiences with his psychotic girl-friend, which he had split off prior to counselling. The crisis intervention patient started to integrate her psychically damaging, ambivalent relationship with her mother. The patient given brief psychotherapy was able to see for the first time essential factors in his relationship with his girl-friend, his mother, and his father that had unconsciously affected his behaviour before this juncture.

The first thing that made such progress possible was the fact that the therapist took his patients' experiences seriously. His sympathetic interest indicated to the patients that their experiences are significant. In psychodynamic terms, we might say that the therapist's interest initiated a psychic cathexis of initially unstructured experiences by reducing anxiety, encouraging self-reflection, and relieving strain on the superego.

Against the background of such psychodynamic assumptions, we can establish on the basis of the hermeneutic principle of "acquisition of otherness in verbal exchange" that a creative, hermeneutic strategy in counselling and psychotherapy consists in empathizing with and thinking one's way into the internal and external experiences of the patient. This interest is of a special kind. Unlike ordinary, everyday sympathy, the interest of the counsellor or therapist is not purely personal. What it does is to situate the client or patient in the context of their own lives by means of the vicarious perceptive work done by the counsellor or therapist.

Another difference over and above ordinary everyday exchanges is the fact that the therapist systematically replicates in his own self the experiences of the client or patient with their own worlds, and then enriches the perceptions of the client with his own views and perspectives on the subject. This happens to a certain degree in other constellations too, but not in this systematic and unilateral form, in which one participant (the counsellor or therapist) places at the disposal of the other participant (the client or patient) his full perceptive competence under controlled conditions.

A counsellor or therapist systematically drawing upon hermeneutic principles for the perception of significant aspects of the client/patient and his/her world, will not interpret these on the basis of a psychological theory. Rather, as we have seen in the case histories, he will first of all indicate to his client, *vis-à-vis* invisible aspects of his or her feelings, actions and experiences in their own personal surroundings. Let me stress once again that these indications are visual. It is *interpretation* in the original meaning of the German word for it (*deuten*): enabling someone to *see*.

If I have attached especial importance to the empathic perceptual attitude of counsellors and therapists, this is because it is a skill that requires painstaking application and cultivation. Counsellors and therapists need to take an interest in the respective worlds of their clients and patients, and to be able to re-enact their experiences in a "mental theatre" of their own devising. In this, counsellors and therapists need a degree of intrepidity in the face of disquieting and unpleasant perceptions. These skills can only be acquired by self-experience, enabling them to face up to unusual aspects of their own emotions and thoughts. In addition, perceptual competence requires a broad interest in the potentialities not only of human failure but also in the myriad possibilities of *structuring*

human existence. Essential to this is not only a profound knowledge of psychological, psychotherapeutic, and psychiatric theories,
but also a keen interest in the different "versions of human existence" as revealed, for example, by art.

Creative imagination

If competent empathy is a relatively unspecific attitude in counselling and psychotherapy, creative imagination in connection with
the picturing of fantasies appears to me to be a psychodynamic
technique that goes beyond everyday exchanges, cognitive behavioural therapy, or Rogers' (1957) client-centred therapy.

As we saw in the case histories, the therapist will generate a
graphic representation of aspects of the patient in his own mind.
These images—timorous little boy exposed to a merciless analytic
gaze, sad/angry little girl who has thrown her doll away, lonely
child longing for a tabooed father—are guiding lines for his psychotherapeutic efforts. In accordance with the second hermeneutic
principle—representational and narrative shaping—the therapist
moves consciously into a scenic, visual world representing essential
aspects of the interaction between the patient and his world.

In contrast to cognitive behavioural therapy, the therapist does
not adhere to an experimentally validated theory or a previously
established disorder model that he finds confirmed in the patient in
one of its different guises and then proceeds to apply. Quite the
contrary. The therapist attempts to free himself of his own experiences and the theoretical stances he may happen to espouse. And
he does so with a view to being as open as possible for the scenic
images projected by the patient. There is no necessity to explain
these in terms of a theory. Psychic products of this nature are in
themselves an attempt to structure what at first is diffuse and
alarming. This is not only something we know from clinical experience, it is also susceptible of theoretical substantiation with the aid
of philosophical hermeneutics and its views on presentational
symbols, transitional phenomena, and the aesthetic constitution of
coherent experience of the world.

The therapist's ability to engage vicariously in fantasy processes
on the patient's behalf requires a predisposition in this direction, a

specific gift, and years of experience. This latter can best be achieved in the framework of creative psychoanalysis, as here the main emphasis of the perceptual attitude is on internal scenic visualizations. The interactive constellation in (successful) psychoanalysis can also assure the distinction between significant images and pointless aestheticizations. A further option is to cultivate this capacity for visual, scenic imagination in the process of everyday fantasy formation or in the active engagement with works of art.

Interactional reflection

In the case histories, I indicated that an essential hermeneutic feature of psychotherapeutic work consists in the therapist's ability to experience the patient's interactions as representations in his own mind. He not only sees the intimidated young man, the sad little girl, and the pining boy, but also attempts to see the persons they relate to and, over and above that, to imagine how these persons interact.

In line with the hermeneutic concept of subjective experience, I have called this systematic representation of intersubjective events interactional experience. We can, thus, define the cultivation of interactional reflection as the third hermeneutic intervention strategy.

In terms of this game theory of psychotherapeutic action, interactional reflection as a principle underlying counsel and therapy means that the therapist first of all maps out vicariously an intrapsychic game with important reference persons on the patient's behalf. This requires readiness on the therapist's part to ingest the relational constellations imparted to him by the patient with all their affective colourings, and to play through them.

This is a complicated matter and it may help to draw the analogy with early interaction between mother and child. The child is not simply "there", it does not tell the mother in so many words how it feels and what it needs. Instead, it is represented by the mother in her own emotional world and in her fantasies, frequently at an unconscious level. On the basis of her own feelings and fantasies, she can then respond spontaneously and appropriately to the needs of the child represented in her own mind.

Interactional reflection is an emotionally challenging task requiring special readiness and competence on the part of the therapist. To sustain the right balance between vicarious interactional experience and his own integrated internal world, the therapist not only needs perceptual competence and the capacity for representational structuring but also adequate distance to keep his involvement with the patient's affective interactional structurings at an emotionally bearable level. This "stand-back" capacity necessary for hermeneutic understanding is termed therapeutic ego-splitting in psychoanalytic terminology. It refers to the necessity of reconciling the capacity for involvement with the capacity for discursive reflection on the psychodynamic events.

In this respect, the counsellor or therapist applying hermeneutic principles needs not only a rich fund of experience of himself and the world, but also—and crucially—extensive clinical experience and theoretical reflection on his own activities. Later, I shall describe disorders where hermeneutic techniques and even a hermeneutic approach are counter-indicated. Recognizing these counter-indications is absolutely essential for counsellors or psychotherapists working with hermeneutic principles.

I shall now discuss how the creative operative principles take effect in counselling and coaching.

CHAPTER SEVEN

Creative principles of counselling and coaching

After the description of the points that counselling and psychotherapy have in common, it is now time to outline some distinctions between them. The most obvious difference is that counselling is not addressed to persons who assess themselves as *psychically ill*. Second, counselling clients display impairments that are not regarded by experts as clinically relevant disorders. But there are major overlaps between the two criteria. Categorization into psychically sound and psychically sick is no easy matter, and the discussion about the specific discrimination between counselling and the psychotherapeutic concept of illness is as old as counselling and psychotherapy themselves. The problems of clear discrimination are highlighted by the fact that many people with minor impairments seek psychotherapy in the interests of their personal development, while many persons with severe disorders would never so much as countenance the idea of asking for psychotherapeutic help. Despite these disclaimers, it is entirely feasible in practice to distinguish counselling cases from therapy cases. Essential determining factors are the concerns of the clients/patients and the extent of their personal and social impairments.

We can define psychological counselling as a scientifically grounded, circumscribed provision of aid in various areas designed to lead to more adequate problem-solving. While it does not serve to remedy psychic disorders, it can have a salutary effect on them. The aims of professional psychological counselling are as manifold as the spheres in which it is offered: educational counselling, family counselling, life counselling, career counselling, etc. In the last few years, the broad range of psychosocial counselling offers has been joined by a new variety specifically aimed at the professional and vocational sphere: coaching.

In the face of global competition, job insecurity, and constant professional and personal change management, the need for counselling in corporate enterprises, social and academic institutions, for managers, politicians, media people, artists, and freelance workers has grown continually over the last few years. Since the 1980s the term "coaching" has established itself for the individual and psychological counselling of individuals and work groups. Coaching is defined as a form of counselling that brings about a synergistic harmonization of the goals of individual personalities and the organizations they work for. It is a combination of psychological counselling, training in specific skills, and personal support. The word "coach" is not, of course, new in itself. It can be traced back at least as far as the nineteenth century when it started being used to designate people at universities in Britain and America whose job it was to prepare and train others for academic tasks, examinations, and sports contests.

Later, large companies placed coaches at the disposal of their managers and executives as confidential consultation partners. Today coaching has extended its purview to middle and junior management. In conflict situations, freelance workers have also increasingly taken to seeking the advice of coaches. Coaching is especially prominent in areas notable for swift development and major change. There appears to be increasing awareness of the fact that professional performance hinges not least on personal development, and that this development can be professionally enhanced. The most usual form in companies is individual coaching by external advisers. Team coaching, project coaching, and coaching by superiors are less widespread forms. However, there are sceptical voices to be heard querying the validity of surveys and the euphoric assessments of coaching success, and dismissing many coaches as charlatans. The least that can be said is that it is a highly variegated field of activity. In the year 2000 there were over 50,000 coaching offerings on the internet. There are no binding quality criteria for coaching, nor any reliable and independent evaluation studies. Typical coaching strategies combine the communication of the coach's personal life philosophy with behavioural training and emotional reinforcement. But there also exist theoretically elaborated and practically evaluated concepts. Obholzer (1996), for example, applies well-established psychodynamic concepts to the realm of coaching.

Among the most successful coaching enterprises are the Ken Blanchard Companies. In their internet presentation (2001) they declare their intention to be the leading provider of solutions encouraging human values and personal development at the workplace. Coaching, they claim, helps people to make optimal use of their abilities and cultivate their well-being. This, in its turn, helps companies to be more successful in confronting the changes that modern society brings with it: "Coaching is a process of self-leadership and helps clients to gain clarity on who they are, what they are doing, and where they are going."

In the book *Everybody is a Coach* (2000), written in conjunction with the most successful trainer in the history of American football, Don Shula, Ken Blanchard reveals the five "secrets" of successful coaching: clarification and realization of convictions and goals; aspiration to professional and personal excellence; commitment to lifelong learning; striving for authenticity; total and unconditional honesty. These objectives and instructions reflect the author's personal view of the world, his fundamental religious convictions, and his life experience, complemented by knowledge about the essentials of successful training.

Coaching, properly understood, *should* improve personal well-being and enhance professional productivity. It can help prevent burn-out syndrome, substance abuse, and stress-related illnesses. Accordingly, coaches need to possess highly qualified personal, psychological and, occasionally, medical skills. The disadvantages of unprofessional coaching immediately become apparent in inadequate problem analysis. A subliminal rivalry problem poisoning the contact between colleagues cannot be coped with by "positive thinking" or training for a "winner mentality". Nor should one recommend an executive with an incipient alcohol problem to have a few drinks to relax. In the fight against fatigue, demotivation, and burn-out it is essential to distinguish whether the persons involved are suffering from dysfunctional aims, poor time management, personal conflicts, or a biological form of depression.

Like unprofessional problem analysis, the use of eclectic techniques without reference to personality profiles and the individual needs of clients is detrimental. A well-trained coach should have learned to analyse the behaviour of clients, identify communicative and psychic disorders, and make a realistic assessment of clients' personalities with their weaknesses and strengths.

Coaching must be distinguished from other forms of personality development, such as consulting, monitoring, mediation, supervision, and psychotherapy: coaching is an external form of counselling for individuals, teams, and work groups that employs the coach's personal, psychological, and field competencies to enhance the productivity, creativity, health, and personal development of staff members. It focuses on professional performance and is more goal- than cause-orientated. Effective self-management is the supreme goal in coaching.

Five coaching elements have proved to be effective:

- a trusting and personally supportive relationship
- use of cognitive techniques for problem-solving
- training of working and presentation techniques
- improvement of communicative skills and psychodynamic understanding
- enhancement of individual and social resources.

Trusting and supportive relationship

As in counselling in general, the quality of the helping relationship is of decisive moment for the success of coaching. As I have shown earlier, the alliance with a person judged to be helpful is frequently itself the first stage in fighting "demoralization". It then leads to self-actualization, and finally (if the relationship is handled correctly) to a feeling of self-efficacy and authenticity.

Use of cognitive techniques for problem-solving

Coaching can serve to identify and analyse dysfunctional working and relational behaviour. Inappropriate perception and evaluation processes can be corrected by Socratic dialogue. Special cognitive techniques can be used to reduce anxiety and dysfunctional stress. This approach is orientated more to results and action than to the clarification of causes. Of substantial importance are also the individually tailored behavioural counsels on the conduct of clients' lives in general: the right balance between productive work and fulfilling leisure activities, life-style-adjusted diet, sufficient physical activity, etc. As with therapists or doctors, the charismatic status of coaches means that these counsels are accepted more readily than they would be from well-meaning advisers in the clients' everyday environment (partners, friends, family, colleagues).

Training of working and presentation techniques

As coaching normally foregrounds professional productivity and creativity, it attaches major significance to the analysis and improvement of work behaviour. Accordingly, time management, working techniques, detailed work plans, and goal-orientation are guiding concepts in this connection.

Coaches must select from the entire repertoire of behaviour-orientated learning the elements best suited to the needs of their clients. Coaching is frequently required to communicate and present work results in an appropriate form, e.g., in the framework of rhetorical training.

Improvement of communicative skills and psychodynamic understanding

Motivational factors are of major significance for work success and personal development at the workplace. Psychologically trained coaches should not have any difficulty in identifying unconscious blockades to personal development and in removing these in collaboration with the clients. Coaching provides clients with a sounding board for conflicts, as well as for positive emotional, cognitive, and social potentialities. The reflection of intra- and inter-personal problems can lead to more self-confidence. This instils the security imperative for creative work. In group coaching, the understanding and moderation of group dynamic processes is necessary to ensure a relaxed and productive working atmosphere.

Enhancement of individual and social resources

In the coaching process, the orientation to the personal and corpo-rate resources available to the client in his field of work occupy the foreground. Coaching is targeted equally at coping with job demands and the individual's ability to come to terms with those demands. The most important resources for mastering stress situa-tions are

- reliable personal relationships
- confidence in one's own abilities
- stability in conflicts
- understanding one's own situation
- authentic action
- confidence and optimism.

In stress situations, the reinforcement of these resources can prevent an individual from failing in his or her tasks.

From what we have said so far it follows that a coach must pos-sess a variety of personal and psychological skills. In addition to his specialist qualifications he also requires field competence, because the different counselling contexts he is faced with—profit and non-profit organizations, higher and middle management, scientists and academics, freelance workers—all display very different communi-cation structures. Work styles and creativity profiles also differ widely in the various fields and professional domains. Coaches will not be able to perform equally well in all fields and domains. Thus, when selecting coaches it is important to establish not only whether they have the necessary personal and professional qualifications, but also whether they fit in with one's own particular domain and life-style. Ultimately, the client should trust to his own intuition and only hire a coach if a trusting and productive working atmosphere has been established after three to five sessions at the most.

On the counselling side, a *creative attitude* taking account of the hermeneutic principles outlined earlier is beneficial for productive coaching. Here are three cases illustrating the point.

A young singer

The young soprano has acquitted herself successfully in her first international appearances. Her talent is generally considered to be beyond doubt. There is, however, a slight snag. Both her professor at the Conservatory and two renowned critics have told her that in her performances a certain tension communicates itself and prevents her from living up to her true potential. This is the reason why she has followed the recommendation of a composer friend and engaged me as coach.

At our first encounter the singer makes a charming, attractive, and self-assured impression. Under the surface, however, there is a slight feeling of unease that subtly but noticeably impairs her voice production. The initial coaching sessions reveal a specific conflict. Whenever the singer gives herself up entirely to her musical portrayal of a character, she feels that she is getting out of her depth. The autotelic necessity of "letting herself go" in the artistic process causes an anxiety similar to the fear of flying. This indecisiveness is rooted in a fundamental internal conflict. On the one hand, she would like to develop her artistic talent and lead a social life of uninhibited ease. On the other, she would prefer to take up a "caring" profession and work as a doctor or a teacher. This would imply a different life-style with a permanent relationship and children. At first she is unaware of the fact that a decision in favour of such a course would be a decision that would spare her a separation from her mother. She entertains a fantasy of a "sheltered" existence reminiscent of a long tradition represented by her mother and grandmother. Artistic activity, by contrast, appears to stand for loneliness and also a loss of intimacy whenever she goes on stage. For her, the stage is an alien world that demands the eschewal of accustomed security.

In the coaching process it proves easy to build up a reliable personal relationship and induce confidence in her own abilities.

Once this has been achieved we can then move on to the implications involved in the creative process.

First, the client was able to improve the flexibility required in her stage performances by learning to apply a number of specific anchoring techniques. These range from everyday rituals and breathing exercises to fantasies enabling her to feel accompanied and supported by familiar persons. Fantasies of this kind, and the systematic employment of an internal dialogue with friends or her counsellor, make it possible for her to relate associatively and playfully to the songs and arias she is required to interpret and perform. This bolsters her self-assurance and she feels progressively more at home with her own voice, her art, and the world of the stage.

As described above, guidance towards a defined objective is less restricted in artists than it is, say, for engineers. But a fantasy journey divided up into short-, medium- and long-term prospects was also helpful for our singer. The conscious enactment of future potentialities in her fantasy gave her greater freedom to engage with her everyday artistic work. She became more independent and non-conformist. She was no longer constantly on the look-out for acceptance or rejection by others, a form of behaviour that prevented her from being "at one with herself" at the beginning of coaching. This increase in authenticity also enabled her to "go beyond her own limits", an aspect of creativity described later as "transcendence".

Once the singer had developed more "courage to be herself", her interest in new songs and arias grew and she discovered new potential for her voice production and musical interpretation. Guidance to greater creativity by means of autotelic self-immersion helped her actively to accept originality and curiosity, rather than fleeing the implications of her gifts for reasons of conformity.

This insight into the singer's central conflicts gave the counselling process a depth without which the elements of creative fascination outlined later would have remained ineffective. Of essential importance was the fact that she learned to accept and understand her ambivalence about embracing an artistic profession. The journey into her past, her anxieties and fears, dreams and longings undertaken in the coaching context, led to greater assurance in developing prospects for the future. After ten double sessions, the inner blockades had been noticeably (and audibly) removed. Since then the singer has consulted me about twice a year, as far as her international commitments allow her to do so.

A gifted scientist

"It's all up, I've messed up my probationary lecture, it's the end of my prospects," the young man blurts out, hardly inside the door. He has failed to achieve the success that would entitle him to carry on and go for a junior professorship. "I might just as well take a rope and hang myself." His mentor and senior professor has sent him to me, but "What can you do to help me?" A phone call from his mathematics professor had filled me in on the details. The young man had received a grant from a foundation for the encouragement of the specially gifted. His professor, who knows him well, describes him as "a reliable young man with a great deal of potential." His poor showing in the lecture is "a complete mystery."

The scientist ("Steven") is a tall, very slim young man. Eyes staring, he sits before me, constantly wiping his sweaty palms on his thighs, swaying back and forth on the chair, and generally presenting a highly driven and disturbed picture. To take the tension out of the situation, I ask him first about how he spends his days. At first he is uncooperative ("That's got nothing to do with the lecture") but then he tells me that on a normal day he works from eight in the morning till eleven at night and then watches fantasy or horror videos "to relax". "*Tempora mutantur*," I think to myself, but then venture to cast doubt on the wisdom of his daily routine. "What am I supposed to do, hang around in pubs?" "Not necessarily. How about going to the theatre or watching a movie?" "Yes, but that would only start me brooding again." "What about?" "That I'll never be as good as my sister who just got a professorship. My father's a medical professor and he can't get over how well his daughter's doing at university. I'll never be that good."

I encourage the client to tell me more about his life. He is happy to report about his parents and how supportive they are to him. He has concentrated all his efforts on the exams so as really to do them proud. I ask about his hobbies and interests, and learn that Steven is a passionate swimmer and that he has always felt very much at ease in the water. I advise him to go swimming once a day in situations of tension, and he agrees to do so. Then we light on other topics, notably his dreams and longings. As he thinks over his response to my inquiry about his three dearest wishes, I notice that Steven is gradually relaxing. His face eases up, his hands are less convulsive, and sometimes he even gives me a glimpse of a rather subversive humour.

He has taken an interest in coaching, and his verdict is that "it really is remarkable the banalities they try and palm off on you just with some psychological trimmings." Group coaching comes in for specially scathing treatment. "All those cult leaders swarming around on the football pitch—no slur on football." He musters me slyly, as if wondering what team I belong to. I register the fact that he seems to have decided he can trust me, and risk a few candid remarks.

To put it briefly, coaching Steven is not difficult. The first interview establishes a trusting relationship, and at the end of it he says he thinks he can see a glimmer of hope on the horizon. In the following interviews we work out a schedule for his next lectures and a leisure programme. Going swimming regularly with a friend helps him to relax and puts him in "good spirits."

When we discuss his prospects for the future, it becomes apparent that he is apprehensive about setting himself apart from others if he embarks on an academic career. "Then you're on your own and the others won't like you." Steven begins to realize that excellence and commitment arouse envy and jealousy in others. For many gifted people this is a frequent (and frequently unconscious) reason not to live up to their true potential.

We have six sessions in the period prior to Steven's next lecture, in which he acquits himself with flying colours. After his successful application for the post he was after, he is now one of those junior professors debating with themselves whether or not to take up the tempting offers from industry. In difficult situations, he falls back on the imagination techniques he learned during coaching and engages in an inner dialogue with me as his imaginary coach: "The opportunity of talking confidentially to a skilled companion about absolutely anything gave me a lot of security and self-confidence."

After two years, the young man consults me again. His professional career is absolutely satisfactory, he is working at an institute that he could not imagine being any better. What worries him now is his "social phobia", by which he means that he feels incapable of establishing a relationship with a woman. "I've set my sights on one or two," he says, "but I haven't made a hit yet." With a liberal sprinkling of military metaphors he goes on talking about his quest for a partner, adding that if he hasn't found a girl-friend by the time he's thirty-five, he intends to shoot himself.

In his descriptions he makes a very rigid impression and reveals a complex fear of women shot through with violent fantasies. His sister appears to him to be infinitely superior and dominant, and in some strange way "in cahoots" with his father. It becomes evident that Steven's conflicts and social anxieties are bound up with complicated real and fantasized family constellations. The fears and relational problems bound up with this can only be allayed in the course of extended psychodynamic or psychoanalytic therapy.

Team coaching in a company context

A major, internationally successful company has difficulty in motivating its executives to engage in constructive collaboration. Backbiting is rife, and the junior staff are resentful. The secretary of the board ventures to say: "The general mood is venomous, and staff members show an increasing tendency to withdraw their active support for projects. There are quite a few burn-out victims. This is harmful not only for the company but also for the staff members." The board itself has been aware of the uncongenial atmosphere in the company but has failed to find any plausible explanation. One colleague enumerates factual reasons for the detrimental atmosphere, another suggests that "the real fly in the ointment is elsewhere." What is to be done? The chairman of the board agrees to have a coach called in. Two weeks earlier, the chairman had attended a lecture of mine and found me convincing both as a person and in my professional capacity. Accordingly, I am asked to take on the job. I am invited to participate in a leadership seminar, the topic of which is defined as "conflict management."

The seminar takes one day and is attended by twenty staff members. I begin with a culture–historical talk on aggression, conflict development, and conflict settlement. Then two groups are asked to prepare a "for and against" discussion on the ideas presented in the talk. The preparations centre around the increasingly technological nature of work modes, leading to overstrain, isolation, loss of quality of life, and ultimately to performance drain for the staff members. The thesis derived from this is that companies must do more for the mental and physical well-being of their employees. The opposing thesis is that entrepreneurial success means an enhancement in the quality of life of staff members. Peace of mind, health, and a cultivated life-style are private matters that a company should not have anything to do with.

The group divides into two sub-groups of ten, subsequently engaging in a dispute in which they attempt to marshal convincing arguments for the respective theses and put those arguments across with maximum rhetorical effect. The dispute itself is fought out between two groups of three delegates, the others are commenting observers.

The results of the seminar can be summed up as follows: initially, not all of the members of each group are willing to espouse the thesis allotted to them. After they are instructed to stand up for the thesis even if it does not square with their personal opinions, counter-arguments recede into the background and all the participants put forward cogent arguments in defence of "their" position.

In the dispute between the two groups of three, the various different communication styles become apparent: conciliatory, moralistic, forthright, competent, authoritative. Video recordings confront them individually with their conflict settlement strategies. The participants can immediately "see through" the roles they are accustomed to adopting or into which they are manoeuvred by the others. In a constructive working atmosphere, all of them complete the seminar with a positive impression of the proceedings. In the anonymous evaluation the following points are emphasized:

- assurance of the coach transmitted to the group as a whole (helping relationship)
- respectful dealings with the individual participants (personal reinforcement)
- acquisition of talk-and-listen techniques for conflict settlement (active coping)
- engagement with pressing problems of the group (understanding and communication)
- "laid back", humorous attitude to the task in hand (actuation of resources).

Such a seminar will be satisfactory for all those involved if the coach is able to implement the general principles of counselling, and to establish and sustain a concentrated, respectful, and fair atmosphere throughout the proceedings. Personally, I reject the kind of approach that touches briefly on controversial topics and indulges the dubious predilection for short-term effects. In my view, the task of the coach throughout the seminar is to ensure that the participants experience the whole event as understanding, helpful, personally reinforcing, problem-settling, and generally productive.

Shortly afterwards, a number of the participants approach me with a request for individual coaching. In the initial interviews, they mention that they are impressed by the positive changes the seminar has already brought about. They now wish to go in search of better ways of coping with stress, and remaining authentic and self-possessed in conflict situations. A few sessions are enough to reveal some very individual problems. Here are four examples of such conflict zones:

- quick professional success leads to difficulties with the home background; fear of jealousy on the part of those left behind; guilt at having left the "native" milieu
- "ageing" and delegation of responsibility; coping with fears of being "shunted into a siding" and forgotten
- over-commitment, feelings of having to be "everywhere at once" so as not to miss out on anything; permanent stress with self and others
- isolation and inner solitude through concentration on work and success.

These conflicts are embedded in different life stories and situations. They proved susceptible of solution by the brief, but intense application of the hermeneutic principles of communication. Due to the more confidential atmosphere, individual coaching allows for a much more personalized approach than group coaching.

To encourage creativity in working groups and individuals the acronym **fascination** may serve as a guideline:

Flexibility and receptiveness for new experiences are essential aspects of creativity. With differences of emphasis in different domains, flexibility is important both in the cognitive and the emotional sphere. Like all the following characteristics and attitudes, flexibility can only contribute to creativity in conjunction with the others.

Associative thinking is something for which Einstein was remarkable even in his early schooldays. In the self-absorption induced by play, he was "as clever and systematic as he was dreamy" (Fölsing, 1995, p. 29). In the arts, free associative thinking plays a crucial role. But science, too, calls for lateral thinking and emotional intelligence. If it degenerates into mere "wool-gathering", however, associative thinking can be an obstacle to productive realization. Then, communication with a counsellor can bring about the requisite balance between creative illumination and creative implementation. The success of a research group or a business enterprise hinges crucially on the ability to turn the creative illumination of the individual into productive and goal-orientated realization.

Self-assurance can be threatened by the specific intensity of creative labour. The creative individual, whether in the guise of Prometheus or of the "mad scientist", breaks loose from the ties of everyday existence. Original thinkers frequently suffer from the loss of accustomed security, they are literally "out of place". This can lead to self-doubt, a phenomenon reported by even the most radiantly creative. They develop various techniques to combat these gnawing doubts, one of them being strict work rituals.

Consistency of purpose distinguishes most creative minds. Even if an author is immersed in a creative game with his or her own self, he or she will be none the less tenacious in the pursuit of creative production. All agree that the creative moment is only vouchsafed to those who devote themselves patiently to their labours. Einstein said:

> Incidentally, I am fully aware that my gifts are nothing special. Curiosity, obsession, and obstinate tenacity, combined with self-criticism, have produced the thoughts I have. (*ibid.*, p. 19)

Intelligence, the ability to make the right decisions, is a crucial factor in creativity. Astonishingly enough, beyond an intelligence quotient of 120 there is no correlation between higher intelligence and greater creativity. Emotional intelligence, motivation, and staying power are essential characteristics making cognitive intelligence fruitful.

Non-conformism is frequently apparent in artists at an early age. Many scientists also display a sceptical attitude to conventional convictions. Of the fourteen-year-old Albert Einstein we are told that he

> never belonged wholeheartedly to his country, his home, his friends, not even to his closest family, but always felt an unremitting sense of alienation *vis-à-vis* such attachments and a need to be alone. [*ibid.*, p. 39]

Creative self-doubt frequently leads to insecurity; reluctance to address these shadowy aspects frequently involves inhibitions to creativity.

Authenticity, the feeling of being able to make a meaningful contribution while retaining full personal responsibility, is a central facet of creativity. Authenticity requires independence and the ability to be alone. This is not always readily distinguishable from unproductive eccentricity. Communication of the results of one's efforts is then especially important for certainty about the quality of authorship.

Transcendence. Acknowledgment of values that go beyond selfish needs is an essential precondition for creativity. Engagement with supra-individual influences is an internal necessity for artists. Paul Valéry (1894) suggests that in science and art we seek a transcendent experience that transforms disorder and chaos into structure.

Interest and "autotelic dedication" are further keys to productivity and creativity. Creative people are able to dedicate themselves totally to a given task over periods of time. In his early youth, Einstein had a profound interest in his "sacred geometry book", whose clarity and certainty made an indescribable impression on him. Such enthusiasm goes hand in hand with a devotion to a given task that has its objective in creative activity itself, not in the results of it.

Originality, like non-conformism, is not only a positive value; it can be a threat to the established and the proven. "Creative destruction" can be disturbing and endanger the psychic balance of the creative mind.

Novelty and curiosity are expressions of a living spirit but will only lead to creative achievement in conjunction with the other aspects listed here. It is in the interplay of the new and the well-established that the nature of creativity reveals itself. To a large degree it is quite simply a mystery, and needs to be respected as such.

CHAPTER EIGHT

The creative aspect of brief dynamic psychotherapy

Psychotherapeutic approaches termed "psychodynamic" proceed on the assumption that feeling, thinking, and acting are influenced by unconscious drives, motivations, fantasies, and interactional experiences. If we listen to them closely, we will find that, over and above their symptoms and disorders, patients enlisting professional psychotherapeutic assistance usually actualize the desire to discover hidden emotional resources, ideas opening up new perspectives, and hitherto unexploited opportunities for action. This discovery is not only achieved in long-term psychoanalysis. Frequently, counselling and brief psychodynamic approaches can produce satisfactory results.

Sigmund Freud, the doyen of psychoanalysis and initiator of a whole range of modern psychotherapeutic approaches based on it, frequently engaged in psychotherapeutic counselling and short-term therapies. In the following, I illustrate how the hermeneutic principles I have described may have taken effect in the earliest account that we have of a case of counselling (or short-term therapy) conducted by Freud.

"Studies on hysteria" (1895) contains a description of Katharina, an eighteen-year-old girl suffering from anxiety and somatization.

One day, when out on a walk during his holiday in the mountains, Freud is asked by Katharina, who is working as a maid in an alpine hut, to grant her an interview. She describes her symptoms to Freud as a compound of shortness of breath, feelings of suffocation, and attacks of extreme anxiety causing her mortal fear. Rather than engaging in a symptom-centred inquiry, Freud's crucial intervention is to encourage the young lady to imagine the situation that triggers her anxieties and "to tell her story". By putting her memories in verbal terms, Katharina is able for the first time to actualize a traumatic situation, and with it the affects initially banished from her psychic *ambiente*. The description of this situation—she has witnessed sexual intercourse between her uncle and a servant girl, and there are also a series of sexual traumatizations she herself has experienced—does not serve to enable the doctor to identify the causes of his patient's symptoms and then to elucidate these to her. The striking thing about Freud's approach—and this is essential to my argument here—is that he does not offer Katharina any explanations or interpretations. His main concern is to organize their exchange in such a way that Katharina feels secure and can then proceed to a visualization of what has occurred, as this has so far eluded perception at the psychic level. Alongside the establishment of a situation that gives the patient security, the main salutary effect of this exchange appears to result from the way it enables Katharina to face up in her conscious psychic *ambiente* something that has been split off and has taken on a life of its own in her unconscious. This is a realization of the principles of memory and narrative shaping. The counsellor's or therapist's function is to provide the patient with a neutral and trustful setting in which she can imagine her psychic (and real) drama and then work on it. In addition, Katharina also finds representation and inclusion in Freud's mental world. This representation reflects the interactional experience of the patient. Thus, she is able for the first time to engage in a relationship with hitherto split-off aspects of her life-world by following the memorial structuring of interactional experience by her interlocutor.

In Freud's account, the opening-up of a space for imagination and visualization led at least to a momentary liberation of the patient from her symptoms. In the text, Freud's own psychodynamic explanation that Katharina's symptoms were rooted in an incestuous desire fended off by means of a conversion neurosis sounds very much like an after-thought. It does not appear to have had any major impact on the success of the treatment. Freud's description of the treatment sequence makes no mention whatsoever of the transference–counter-transference process.

We also have accounts of Freud's approach to counselling and brief psychotherapy from the patients' viewpoint. Famous among these is the four-hour interview requested by the composer and conductor Gustav Mahler because of the profound conflicts assailing him. His wife Alma Mahler-Werfel reports (1960) on the positive effects of this long exchange and the notable improvement it effected on the psychic difficulties Mahler was plagued by. The conductor Bruno Walter (1940) refers to a course of treatment comprising six sessions with Freud, which successfully remedied the paralysis in his right arm. Unfortunately, we know too little about the principles underlying these sessions and the intervention strategies employed.

Implicitly, Freud engaged on many occasions with the approaches derived from psychoanalysis. Explicitly, in "Advances in psycho-analytic therapy" (1919), he addressed the prospects of wide-ranging psychotherapeutic care for large sectors of the population:

> When this happens, institutions or out-patient clinics will be started, to which analytically-trained physicians will be appointed, so that men who would otherwise give way to drink, women who have nearly succumbed under their burden of privations, children for whom there is no choice but between running wild or neurosis, may be made capable, by analysis, of resistance and of efficient work. Such treatments will be free. [. . .] We shall then be faced by the task of adapting our technique to the new conditions. [1919, p. 167]

Although this vision can now be said to have been realized in part, the "adaptation to new conditions" appears to present a problem. The elaboration of applied psychoanalytic approaches and the integration of cognitive, behaviour-orientated procedures is still at a rudimentary level. Freud's own view was that the psychoanalytic quest for truth would be hampered by integrative approaches. His sceptical evaluation of the situation is frequently cited.

It is very probable, too, that the large-scale application of our therapy will compel us to alloy the pure gold of our analysis freely with the copper of direct suggestion. [1919, pp. 167–168]

But in the same article Freud also contends that of all the practical approaches he considers urgently necessary, the best will be derived from classical analysis.

But, whatever form this psychotherapy for the people may take, whatever the elements out of which it is compounded, its most effective and most important ingredients will assuredly remain those borrowed from strict and untendentious psycho-analysis. [1919, p. 168]

What Freud is saying here, in effect, is that exclusively charismatic and manipulative styles of counselling and psychotherapy are not compatible with the emancipatory claims of psychoanalysis.

In the wake of Freud, brief psychotherapy models were elaborated, justified notably by their short duration and the provision of psychotherapy for large sectors of the population. As early as 1911, Wilhelm Stekel, a pupil of Freud's, began conducting counselling and short-term therapy on a psychoanalytic basis. He systematized his experiences in a book entitled *Techniques of Analytic Psychotherapy* (1938). In it he advocated a temporally and thematically restricted technique that did not set out to engage with infantile conflicts and the full scope of their effects. In 1918, Ferenczi, another of Freud's pupils, embarked on the development of "active therapy". His proposal was to actively confront patients suffering from phobias or compulsive neuroses with their anxiety or phobia. The main objective for the therapeutic situation, however, was to pay special attention to the emotional experience of the patient. By concentrating on the patients' feelings and modes of subjective experience in the here-and-now, it should be possible to simplify and shorten psychoanalytic therapies. Additionally, the time limit was regarded as a special opportunity for working on separation conflicts (Ferenczi & Rank, 1924).

Central to the therapeutic proposals made by Alexander and French (1946) was the idea of "therapeutic flexibility". They suggested sessions of different frequency depending on individual needs, longer or shorter intervals in the overall course of treatment, and combinations with other forms of therapy. As this "experimenting with the setting" displayed some markedly manipulative features, severe criticism of the proposals was voiced. However, this did little to influence the development of short-term psychoanalytic therapies. Notably their concept of "corrective emotional experience" can be a major factor in the therapeutic encounter, enabling the patient to query and change habitual views and behaviours.

Other pioneers in the field of counselling and brief dynamic psychotherapy were Enid and Michael Balint (1961), who succeeded in applying counselling techniques based on psychoanalysis in the medical professions. In addition, they elaborated a detailed concept of focal therapy. In 1973 Balint described his treatment of a forty-three-year-old patient with a marked jealousy paranoia, of which he was cured in the course of twenty-seven sessions (Balint et al., 1973).

Inspired by Balint, David Malan (1963) started systematizing brief psychoanalytic therapies in a therapeutic team, with a view to validating the results at a later date. Malan developed a stringent, brief-therapy design, emphasizing the interpretation of the here-and-now in the therapeutic relationship, and limiting treatment to between ten and fourteen sessions. In so doing, he was placing the emphasis on the transference situation in a way familiar from psychoanalysis. With this procedure, Malan claimed to be able to effect extensive improvements not only in the symptoms but also in the neurotic behaviours of patients with relatively extensive and long established neuroses. Indication and prognosis, he said, depended upon whether the patient was capable of responding to the focusing of his conflicts and reacting positively to the interpretations of the therapist in the first few sessions. The most striking successes were achieved in therapies where the therapist was "enthusiastic" and emotionally committed. In the last analysis, Malan's design retains its allegiance to the classical psychoanalytic paradigm. The patient's intrapsychic conflict is actualized in the transference process and interpreted with reference to its biographical genesis. He insists that brief therapy is targeted at an unconscious, usually oedipal infantile conflict. Where this isimpracticable, a different "supportive" technique of a non-analytic nature should be given preference.

In contrast to the concern with individually specific conflict dynamics in Malan, J. Mann (1973) centred his counselling and therapeutic efforts around the general problem of coping with separation conflicts. The aim was to achieve greater autonomy and self-respect. With a view to confronting the client or patient with the restricted period of therapy (and ultimately of life itself), the termination of the strictly limited number of twelve sessions is scheduled right from the outset. This procedure claimed to be especially successful with adolescents labouring under separation conflicts between themselves and their parents.

Focal therapy has attained classical status. It limits itself to working on a biographically conditioned conflict by means of its actualization in the patient–therapist relationship. Seen thus, analytic focal therapy could be justly regarded as a shortened form of psychoanalysis.

A change of emphasis is discernible in the work of Davanloo (2001). In contrast to the classical preference for working on resistance, he attempts to address the patients' "vital ego functions" directly. The collapse of resistance, he asserts, leads not to loss of structure and regression but to a notable improvement identifiable, e.g., on the video recordings of the various sessions.

Let us take a new look at the patients in our case histories from the viewpoint of brief dynamic psychotherapy and hermeneutic/creative approaches. In psychodynamic terms, we might describe Anna's destruction of her scope for positive action as a masochistic reaction. Anna has major guilt feelings and can only come to terms with them by making herself suffer and "switching off" emotionally. Such an interpretation would have been entirely plausible. But it would have disrupted the scenic interaction. The fantasies induced in my mind made it possible for me to perceive the happy, then sad little girl, the attractive, then desperate young woman. This helped me to achieve a friendly attitude that Anna was no longer able to assume towards herself. I understood this as the expression of a longing to stay in touch with the vital, living elements of her own self. Perhaps, by way of identification, Anna was able to re-establish that contact with a side of herself that had sprung to life in me although she herself had lost touch with it. It may have been my therapeutic function to structure these aspects of Anna's psyche vicariously for her in my own fantasy. Anna may have perceived this unconsciously, for she told me that our interview had given her some hope and was like "a ray of light on the horizon".

In this crisis intervention, as in the counselling and brief psychotherapy described above, the point at issue is not insight into an elemental conflict such as an Oedipus complex. But more superficial conflict areas are not explicitly interpreted either. With a classical psychoanalytic approach to our case histories, we could, for example, have brought the ambivalence conflicts to light. It seems very likely that essential ambivalence conflicts were in fact worked upon implicitly. But such probabilities cannot be substantiated in the course of time-limited therapeutic interaction, and by extension there is no way of validating them by a working-through.

With equal justification, we could draw upon the ideas of Alexander and French and say that an empathic and trust-enhancing attitude made it possible for the patients to engage with experiences of crucial importance for them and to go through a corrective emotional experience. In Davanloo's terms, we might say that "vital ego functions" of the patient were addressed by the therapist, thus indicating and opening up constructive modes of behaviour. In terms of psychoanalytic procedures in the original sense, however, we can say that no interpretation of "profound" conflicts, let alone of the transference situation, in fact took place. But it is equally true that the patients were still able to use the therapist as a "helpful object". On the basis of images triggered in him by the patient, the therapist was able to pinpoint certain aspects of their inner lives relatively directly. In the psychotherapeutic counselling case, he was able to perceive the patient's need to allow himself a little more freedom and vitality under the protective shelter of a stable authority. In the crisis counselling case, the therapist was able to put the patient back in touch with the active side of her personality that she was unable to establish contact with of her own accord. The images thus enacted placed split-off elements of her psychic life at her disposal again. Much the same happened in the short-term psychotherapy instance.

The hermeneutic version of dynamic psychotherapy also places a different emphasis on the understanding of dreams. The hermeneutic approach is not primarily concerned with the decoding of dreams, although this is still significant. As in modern psychoanalysis, the main point of interest is the function of dreams in imposing a structure on diffusely oppressive material. As in a literary work, the interpretation may be important but it is not always necessary to enable the dream or the work of art to have an effect. The structuring of a fantasy or a dream has an impact of its own without any further interpretation. In this it is similar to the effect of a poem.

Like psychoanalytic techniques, hermeneutic–creative intervention strategies seek to identify unconscious experience that, despite its significance and its effect on behaviour, is both unconscious and inaccessible to the individual, and to put it back at his or her disposal. The most prominent differences are to be found in the following areas:

Perception—interpretation

Creative–hermeneutic interventions aim not at an interpretation of psychodynamic conflicts but at making perception and representation possible in the form of scenic images. The German word for interpretation (*Deutung*) means "pointing at something" and thus reveals the visual aesthetic accent of the perception. By contrast, "interpretation" is more a process of cognitive abstraction.

Narrative shaping—resistance and defence

In counselling and dynamic psychotherapy of the kind I have been describing both in theory and practice, a detailed analysis of resistance plays no part. Resistance is circumvented by way of a relatively direct engagement with the fantasy material provided by the patient, and by quick use of the images taking shape in the therapist's mind. Naturally, care must be taken not to spring the therapist's images on the patient. These have to be offered to the patient in a circumspect way. It is also important that these offerings be identifiable as such; for example, by using formulations such as: "The vision I have at the moment is that of your partner. Might it not be that you would like to show your affection for him . . .".

Interactional experience—transference and counter-transference

In the case histories, no thematic reference was made to transference on to the therapist. While the counsellor or therapist does make use of the transference manifestations in order to understand his client or patient, he refrains from any encouragement or interpretation of the transference situation itself. He does not explicitly address the emotional connection between himself and the client or patient in the here-and-now. Accordingly, the patient's conflicts are not worked through in the therapeutic encounter.

Encouragement of transference and the analysis attendant upon it leads the patient and the therapist into an intensive emotional relationship. In classical psychoanalysis, such a situation is actively aimed at, with a view to pointing up central conflict constellations and enabling the patient to understand things past as things experienced in the present. This requires a specific emotional and cognitive attitude requiring high session frequency and a long period of treatment. Many patients profit from such long-term treatment. For others, however, it is not necessary to carry out a fully-fledged transference–counter-transference analysis, as they are able to draw upon their capacity for "regression in the service of the ego" outside the treatment, say by structured fantasy formation. In everyday life, it is quite normal for people to withdraw into presentational, "dreamy" modes of perception in breaks from work, artistic and creative activity, or in sleep. I have described their structuring and integrative function for our spiritual lives and their necessity for our mental health. In creative counselling and brief psychotherapy, this natural ability is used and encouraged. Avoidance of a transference neurosis is necessary to minimize the patient's dependence on the therapist and to help the patient from the outset of therapy to preserve his capacity for perceptual regression and intrapsychic structuring outside the therapeutic context.

Accordingly, the intention of counselling and brief psychotherapy is to provide the patient with a space for enacting and structuring his or her psychic drama that can be drawn upon outside the treatment setting. From the very outset, and this is a distinguishing factor between this and psychoanalysis, potential for action and structuring in external reality with important reference persons and the autonomous play area in the patient's internal life are the object of psychotherapeutic work. By contrast, psycho-analysis focuses on feelings, ideas, modes of experience, and conflict constellations of the kind actualized *vis-à-vis* the analyst in the transference situation. In cases where, say for lack of time or for financial reasons, psychoanalysis is not feasible, transference mani-festations should be taken note of but not placed at the centre of interpretative work. In fact, we now have empirical indications corroborated by supervision experience that transference–counter-transference interpretations in brief psychotherapy produce detri-mental results (Luborsky *et al.*, 1988). Important as our efforts towards common creative principles for counselling and psychotherapy may be, we need to establish unequivocally that explicit work on transference and counter-transference belongs squarely in the province of psychoanalysis.

CHAPTER NINE

The creative aspect of psychoanalysis

Apart from the more implicit role allotted to transference and counter-transference, creative hermeneutic approaches are elements of dynamic psychotherapy. Accordingly, the distinctions over and against psychoanalysis are fluid. Many psychoanalysts would probably agree that perception/memory, narrative shaping, and interactional experience are essential elements of the analytic approach. The following case history will illustrate this point. It has already been published in modified versions in scientific journals (cf. Holm-Hadulla, 2003). It is the case of a female patient with marked, generalized anxiety and a borderline personality disorder.

A case for psychoanalysis

After two fruitless encounters with psychotherapy, Maria, a young doctor, applies insistently for psychoanalysis. She suffers from pronounced diffuse and phobic anxieties that are increasingly getting in the way of her work and also have a very detrimental effect on the conduct of her personal life. She has broken with her parents and discontinued all contact with her two younger sisters because they are doing well and she envies them for it. The two previous contacts with psychotherapy were (a) psychodynamic and (b) behaviour therapy. In both cases, Maria caused her therapists considerable difficulty. She would regularly contact them at weekends and in her distress would also phone them late at night. Her therapists gave her soothing tapes and literature to take home with her and permitted contact outside the regular appointments, but the treatment sessions became more and more arduous. Maria herself criticizes these "favours" and the behaviour-therapeutic interventions because they only reinforced her insecurity, lack of independence, and lack of structure. Ultimately, her complaints became more and more intolerable and she could hardly control her thoughts of suicide.

> In our preliminary interviews, Maria not only arouses a desire in me to help her, she also arouses my curiosity about the chances she has of achieving personal development despite the pronounced intensity of her symptoms. But at the beginning of therapy she displays features that are both threatening and threatened. Maria causes me very considerable worry and concern. The vital and appealing side of her nature and the verbal dexterity that she demonstrated at the preliminary interviews, despite her deep-seated anxieties, rapidly give way to thoroughgoing helplessness and diffuse tension. In the first sessions Maria restricts our exchanges to the subject of the suicidal tendencies she has been entertaining for some time now, and mentions the impulse she feels to follow the example of a friend of hers and throw herself in front of a train. She suggests that the only real protection she can find is in a psychiatric hospital. As if to allay the fears and the concern that is gradually taking hold of me, she begins to idealize me and generates an eroticized atmosphere in the sessions. In crass contrast to this, she denigrates me to her friends, and starts investigating my life in search of dark spots. Then again, she stylizes herself as a helpless child, feels powerless, and believes that she is the object of rejection on my part. Maria attacks the setting, and I have difficulty keeping the analytic framework stable in the face of her desire to call me outside the hours, and to arrange for special appointments in times of crisis. She is sorely afraid that she might lose me, that I might fall ill or die. My initial impressions are fragmentary and imageless, devoid of reality. Strangely, I have difficulty listening to the patient with the necessary attention, I retain little of what she tells me, and can neither understand nor recall the associations and the dreams she tells me about.

After the first holiday break, it all comes bursting out. During those weeks she has felt desperate, paralysed, sometimes as if she were dead. Now, immediately before my return, she had been completely mixed up, completely preoccupied with me, she had seen my face everywhere and been unable to distance herself at all from this mysterious, uncanny bond that united us. She is unable to "think straight" and feels powerless to do anything about it. She has only been able to suppress the urge to phone me or seek assistance from colleagues of mine because she was afraid that this would arouse my disapproval. As Maria tells me all this in a frankly irate tone of voice, she conveys a diffuse impression of anxiety, profound alarm, and also annoyance. I begin to doubt whether I can keep her in psychoanalysis.

Suddenly, very concrete images of abortions present themselves to my inward eye. As I explore my own fantasies and memories of painful experiences, my confusion begins to resolve itself as a result of internal scenic images. I am now able to tell Maria "that your rage and disappointment with me has led to an impulse on your part to destroy what is taking shape here between us, the fruits of our labour." After a brief silence, she tells me in an entirely different tone of voice that she has just had an extremely graphic vision: "A baby is being slaughtered above me. Absolutely awful, monstrous." I say: "Perhaps your need to protect me means that you have to get rid of yourself before it is too late and attack what is growing inside you."

Maria falls silent for a moment, then says that she has a great longing for me. A dividing partition between us has fallen. She recalls a distressful scene. When she was a small child, she was very frail and indefinably sick. Just before her third birthday she had to be committed to hospital and it seemed very likely that she might die. Her parents were not allowed to approach her bed and had to stay outside. She remembers that on her return home after three weeks in hospital she had spoken only to her father, and this in perfect High German. She had been unwilling to recognize her mother. This memory indicates to Maria that she wanted to eradicate and exterminate both herself and my receptiveness because of the pain and rage caused by the separation. Her tendency to consign a misshapen, ailing treatment to the rubbish bin and at best to engage in a coquettish encounter with me as a male partner was the expression of vengeance for the inadequate reception she felt she had been given by her mother, which she intended to castigate (in the psychoanalytic re-enactment) with the full force of her contempt. On the other hand, Maria inspired in me images and fantasies I was able to follow up in her presence. I interpreted this as an attempt at reparation

on the part of the patient, serving to keep me well-disposed and interested. In this connection, Maria discovered her promiscuous and
manipulative attitude to men as the displacement and attempted reparation of a painful disappointment caused by the realization that a good
and stable maternal introject was very difficult for her to retain.

In the further course of analysis, Maria fantasizes herself as a greedy
and gluttonous little child robbing her mother of the last ounce of
vitality, and also draining me to the core in the context of the therapy.
At the same time, she is able to relish the fact that she generates
fantasies in me that are structured into interpretations. The acceptance
of her reparatory tendencies, the establishment of a relationship to the
child within that takes what it needs and thus bestows gratification on
her reference persons, is an important experience for Maria. At a different level—Maria dreams that she is standing outside my house which
is surrounded by a big park and has a magnificent gate outside it, but
then finally elects to skulk around outside my rear entrance to find out
what comes out—she is engaging with her fear that the things she puts
into me might come back out at her undigested, as destructive material. On the other hand, the patient dreams that there is something
"quite wonderful" concealed in the vicinity of the rear entrance. Later,
in her dreams and ideas, Maria engages with herself as a lively but
needy child. At the same time she is the adult, instinct-driven woman
for whom the child is a nuisance. She dreams: "I have a little child, a
baby. Suddenly I'm somewhere entirely different with another adult
person and I say to myself: 'My God, how could I leave the child on its
own?' Then my girl-friend says: 'Why are you so worried? Your
father's looking after the child.' But in the dream I have the feeling that
I must make up for something, I have to go back, I don't know whether
I can ever make good that breach of faith."

Maria finds it difficult to tolerate the fact that something is taking shape
jointly that she cannot achieve on her own. Fantasies about our shared
fertility involve her in oedipal guilt feelings about being her father's
favourite and gutting the mother with her predatory attacks. This is
illustrated by her guilty, ambivalent desire to supplant my other female
patients in my favour. On the couch she is able to experience emotionally and graphically how angry and disappointed her reaction is to the
locked bedroom door and the door to my surgery, how impotent and
vindictive she is in the face of the intensive fascination and the name-
less dread that befalls her in this connection. She gives a vivid description of the malicious vengeance she will take, as if she were the little
three-year-old who will soon show the mother who is going to get all

the attention. In her fantasy she rehearses a sado-masochistic form of tyranny in which she frightens and threatens me, but at the same time feels depreciated and badly treated by me. For the first time she is able to recognize it as her own. Parallel to this psychoanalytic awareness of these conflicts, the patient also succeeds in enjoying the material fruits and the recognition accorded to her professional work, and separates herself from her doctoral dissertation (a "nuisance" to her) by bringing it to a successful end.

The stark actualization of conflicts sometimes tends to cover up the other aspects of therapy, the silent, covert effects it can have. This can be illustrated by the development of one of the patient's symptoms. At the beginning of analysis, Maria was suffering from attacks of asthma that required medication. A few weeks into the treatment, she inadvertently left her antiasthma spray in my surgery. After this incident her respiratory disorder disappeared. Obviously the patient was able to use the analytic situation as a relationship that made the symptom superfluous. Only two years later, when she was pregnant and necessarily engaged with her role as mother, did she recall that when she was about eight years old she went into her mother's bed when she had a nocturnal attack of asthma and this invariably got rid of it. This suggests that the patient was able to use the psychoanalytic situation as a supportive matrix and a transitional space where she could structure her psychic drama without having recourse to the concretistic objectification in the form of a psychosomatic symptom.

Finally, I want to recall the hermeneutic aspects of this multi-faceted case history. My opinion is that the hermeneutic principles of memory, representational structuring, and interactional experience were crucial for the success of the treatment. In the psychoanalytic situation they are applied in a highly concentrated way. Despite all the malicious criticism psychoanalysis is attracting at the moment, it cannot be said often enough that for many patients it is still the best form of psychotherapeutic treatment.

Psychoanalytic concepts of creativity

In Freud's interpretation of dreams, the creativity of ordinary persons is the focus of concern. The mechanisms of dream-work—

condensation, displacement, concern for representability, and secondary revision—create the manifest dream content out of the latent dream thoughts and can be legitimately regarded as a creative process. Dream images demand to be understood as aesthetic structurings blending the unconscious with the conscious, fantasy with reality, and primary with secondary processes. They are also essential elements of parapraxis (1901), jokes (1905), and aesthetic shaping (see below).

The mechanisms described in "The interpretation of dreams"— notably condensation and displacement—are the expression of an unconscious desire. Freud himself was cautious about comparing, let alone equating, the mechanisms of dream-work with the mechanisms of artistic achievement, in the way the surrealists did so extensively. In his later writings, Freud approaches the problem of human creativity by comparing children's play with artistic creativity. "Might we not say that every child at play behaves like a creative writer, in that he creates a world of his own . . ." (1908b, p. 143).

The essential motives for play and creative imagination are coping with reality and realizing drive needs.

> We must not suppose that the products of this imaginative activity—the various phantasies, castles in the air and day-dreams—are stereotyped or unalterable. On the contrary, they fit themselves into the subject's shifting impressions of life [. . .]. Mental work is linked to some current impression, some provoking occasion in the present which has been able to arouse one of the subject's major wishes. From there it harks back to a memory of an earlier experience (usually an infantile one) in which this wish was fulfilled; and it now creates a situation relating to the future which represents a fulfilment of the wish. What it thus creates is a day-dream or phantasy, which carries about it traces of its origin from the occasion which provoked it and from the memory. Thus past, present and future are strung together, as it were, on the thread of the wish that runs through them.

> A very ordinary example may serve to make what I have said clear. Let us take the case of a poor orphan boy to whom you have given the address of some employer where he perhaps may find a job. On his way there he may indulge in a day-dream appropriate to the situation from which it arises. He is given a job, finds favour with

his new employer, makes himself indispensable in the business, is taken into the employer's family, marries the charming young daughter of the house, and then himself becomes a director of the business, first as his employer's partner, then as his successor. In his phantasy, the dreamer has regained what he possessed in his happy childhood—the protecting house, the loving parents and the first objects of his affectionate feelings. You will see from this example the way in which the wish makes use of an occasion in the present to construct, on the pattern of the past, a picture of the future. [1908, pp. 147–148]

Freud coined the term "sublimation" to discuss the way we structure and cope with instinctual impulses. The term evokes both the meaning of "sublime" as "refinement" and as a category of the fine arts, and "sublimation" in the sense of a chemical process. Freud repeatedly uses the concept to refer to a psychic process underlying creative activity, intellectual work, and occupations that are of value to society in some way.

Freud's ambivalence about creative fantasizing becomes apparent in these two quotes:

You will be taught that we humans, with the standards of our civilization and under the pressure of our internal repressions, find reality unsatisfying quite generally, and for that reason entertain a life of phantasy in which we like to make up for the insufficiencies of reality by the production of wish-fulfilments. [1910, S. E., XI, pp. 49–50]

But this idea of wish-fulfilment is immediately set off against the very realistic idea of coping.

These phantasies include a great deal of the true constitutional essence of the subject's personality as well as of those of his impulses which are repressed where reality is concerned. [ibid., p. 50]

This means that fantasy is a way of representing reality. It may remind us of Hegel's definition of the work of art as the "sensuous appearance of the idea" (1812). Behind this is the ideal of a reconciliation of the reality and pleasure principles with which Freud was concerned throughout his life. "The energetic and successful

man is one who succeeds by his efforts in turning his wishful phantasies into reality" (1920, p. 50).

If this work fails "as a result of the resistances of the external
world and the subject's own weaknesses", the individual with-
draws from reality and attempts to establish a more gratifying
fantasy world in his symptoms.

> In certain favourable circumstances, it still remains possible for him
> to find another path leading from those phantasies to reality,
> instead of becoming permanently estranged from it by regressing
> to infancy. If a person who is at loggerheads with reality possesses
> an *artistic gift* (a thing that is still a psychological mystery to us), he
> can transform his phantasies into artistic creations instead of into
> symptoms. In this manner he can escape the doom of neurosis and
> by this roundabout path regain his contact with reality. [*ibid.*]

But Freud still appears to believe in the original creativity of the
ordinary individual. Guided by the basic rule of psychoanalysis,
the patient must notice and report

> whatever comes into his head, not being misled, for instance, into
> suppressing an idea because it strikes him as unimportant or irrele-
> vant or because it seems to him meaningless. He must adopt a
> completely impartial attitude to what occurs to him, since it is
> precisely his critical attitude which is responsible for his being
> unable, in the ordinary course of things, to achieve the desired
> unraveling of his dream or obsessional idea or whatever it may be.
> [1900, p. 101]

Thus Freud here expects enlightenment to be the result not of
systematic obedience of the reality principle but of relaxation and
free association transforming undesired ideas into visual scenes
and other sensuous experiences.

For Freud, creativity is essentially unconscious.

> We are probably inclined greatly to over-estimate the conscious
> character of intellectual and artistic production as well. Accounts
> given us by some of the most highly productive men, such as
> Goethe and Helmholtz, show rather that what is essential and new
> in their creations came to them without premeditation and as an
> almost ready-made whole. [19500, p. 613]

What, then, is Freud's view of the difference between the creativity of an ordinary person and the creativity of an artist? With reference to dreams, Freud indicates that most people are able to produce innovatory fantasies and that dream-work invariably has a creative aspect. The connections this generates are new and frequently surprising. One essential distinction between everyday fantasy and art appears to be that dreams and fantasies are only of minor interest to others. Works of art are fantasies that are accessible to a large number of people through the way in which they are structured.

Jacques Lacan (1975), a thinker influenced by Freud, centres the psychoanalytic understanding of creativity on an existential lack. This *manque primordial* is the source of all creativity. The relationship of man to himself and his own nature is disturbed by an original conflict. This conflict has to do with the prematurity of human birth. The human individual arrives in this world in a state of inadequacy, and Lacan suggests that in the "mirror stage" the individual evades this inadequacy by means of anticipation. I-formation then is like a suit of armour or a fortified camp surrounding the "image of the fragmented body." An essential role in our defence against this *manque primordial* and the feeling of annihilation is played by language as a paradigm of human creativity. Truth has to be constantly re-found, constantly re-produced. Human desire, which finds its meaning in the desire of the other, has to be permanently re-created because it is symbolically structured.

In her concept of creativity, Melanie Klein (1957) initially takes up Freud's theory of sublimation. She emphasizes the connection between creativity and profound early anxieties. Creative impulses, in her view, are grounded in the fact that an object wounded by a destructive attack is reconstituted and thus re-created. From her experiences as a child analyst, Klein concludes that the mother's breast is perceived as creative, and that excessive envy of its bountiful and sustaining nature militates against the child's own creative abilities. Like envy, guilt feelings will also hamper creativity if they are overly pronounced. If infantile anxieties can be overcome, creative impulses will manifest themselves spontaneously in the form of activities such as drawing, making things, handiwork, and language. Destructive impulses are reduced when they are given a structure. If, after the reduction of anxieties and guilt feelings, the child or patient can become receptive to love impulses, a strong desire for reparation ensues, which may find expression in creative and constructive forms (cf. Segal, 1991). The quintessence of Klein's creativity theories is that creativity serves to cope with destructive impulses and allows for an integrated experience of reality through symbolization. This seems to me to be readily compatible with Freud and Lacan. It is not only in the elation and sufferings of artists but also in everyday life-styles that individuals are concerned to achieve a sense of coherence. Bollas (1992) speaks of an almost biological need for imposing and asserting structure.

Donald Meltzer (1988) has differentiated and extended Klein's conception. He locates all the decisive experiences of the psychoanalytic patient—similar to those of the infant with its parents—in the aesthetic province. As patients regress to infantile modes of perception and psychic functioning, new, original, and also threatening aspects of significant others will be borne in on them. The psychoanalyst's job is to perceive and work on these frightening and fascinating sensuous experiences. Initially, discursive thinking is excluded from this area: "There can be no arguing, only evocation". The analyst's activity consists in producing an imaginative re-creation of biographical continuity. In his early psychophysiological model, Freud traced the functions of the "psychic apparatus" and the "ego" to the necessity of protecting oneself from overwhelming stimuli. To emphasize the sensuous and aesthetic factor in structuring for the purpose of impulse protection, or perhaps more accurately impulse processing, Meltzer coins the term "aesthetic conflict". This conflict sheds light on the creative aspect of stimulus protection. From the very outset, intensive stimuli "break in on" the infant. They demand synthesis and a translation into psychic structures. A conflict, in the psychoanalytic sense of the term, will ensue if sensuous experience cannot be creatively structured because of destructive and envious impulses. Meltzer proceeds on the assumption that a "beautiful enough" mother will be an object of overwhelming interest to her "beautiful enough" baby. The aesthetic impression of the "beautiful" mother is accessible to the senses, but her inner being remains mysterious and covert. This is the source of creative imagination. If the envy of the inaccessible inner being of the "beautiful enough" mother (here Meltzer paraphrases Winnicott) becomes intolerable, this will lead to an attack on the entire world of sensuous perception. The enigmatic mother and the aesthetically constituted environment will then provoke not curiosity and creativity, but denial, splitting, and arrested development.

For Heinz Kohut (1971), creative engagement with the internal and external world is an elementary event that transforms archaic into healthy narcissism in a supportive environment. Kohut suggests a close connection between disappointed needs for contact and desires for conjugation that, in the ideal case, will change into a creative, empathic conjugation with the environment. Creativity serves the acquisition of a healthy narcissistic balance. It reconciles the extension of an actively creative self with the desire to derive strength from an idealized object. Successful psychoanalysis, says Kohut, can lead not only to increased empathy and a creative interest in psychic processes beyond the limits of one's own mind, but also to genuinely creative impulses.

We also find the idea of primary creativity in the thinking of Wilfried Bion (1962). Basing his ideas on the concept of projective identification proposed by Melanie Klein, he sees this as the primal form of human communication. From the outset, the infant gathers emotional experience through acoustical, visual, and olfactory sensations that give structure to its psyche. Through interaction with the mother, the infant is able to transform proto-mental thoughts into material for conscious and unconscious thinking. Thus experience begins in the encounter between innate schemata and suitable sensuous experiences. According to Bion, this is a basic model for constructive thinking and creative activity.

CHAPTER TEN

Indications and counter-indications for the creative attitude

B efore I summarize the indications for the creative attitude, I should like to recall the two levels of creative-hermeneutic counselling and psychotherapy.

First, the creative-cum-hermeneutic approach can be regarded as a communicative basis for counselling. Within this basic approach, a number of techniques can be used, from the interventions elaborated by cognitive behavioural approaches to psychodynamic techniques inspired by a long psychoanalytic tradition. To this extent, the basic hermeneutic approach may be regarded as a philosophically and anthropologically substantiated foundation for integrative counselling.

Second, there are problems and psychic disorders where the application of creative and hermeneutic principles are accentuations of dynamic psychotherapy. Let me summarize the essential fields where they can be applied.

The creative attitude in the counselling context

In my experience, creative hermeneutic principles have proved valuable in counselling for various problem areas and conflict situations:

- difficulties at work
- presentation anxiety
- decision-making problems
- leadership problems
- team conflicts
- communication problems
- partnership problems
- development crises

Accordingly, this general mode of understanding and its specific intervention strategies can act as a basic model in the following areas:

- school, study, and career counselling
- professional career counselling
- personnel development
- marriage, family, and upbringing counselling
- general life counselling

Let us recall that the creative hermeneutic approach is not effective on its own but forms the foundation for the integrative application of a wide range of counselling techniques. If clients are unmotivated or reject the approach, the creative hermeneutic attitude is inappropriate to the counselling context.

The creative approach in psychotherapy

Creative hermeneutic therapy as an accentuation of dynamic psychotherapy derives its effect from competent empathy, creative imagination, and interactional perception. These aspects acting in concert serve to activate the resources at the command of our patients. Resources cannot develop before hermeneutic structuring reduces the alien nature of shameful and disquieting experiences active in a suppressed or split-off form, and producing symptoms or inappropriate behaviour. The psychodynamic and psychoanalytic forms of therapy based on hermeneutic principles have proved their clinical value in dealing especially with the following psychic disorders:

- adjustment disorders
- anxiety disorders
- affective disorders
- eating disorders
- personality disorders.

As in counselling, the creative hermeneutic approach and the intervention strategies associated with it are not effective on their own. They are always incorporated into an overall treatment plan geared to the respective person, his or her social/cultural environment, and his or her disorder.

An indication for psychotherapy with a hermeneutic slant cannot be established on the basis of the assessment of problems or of the diagnosis alone. It is much more important to use the first sessions to assess whether the patients are reacting positively to the psychotherapeutic encounters. A gauge of this is whether or not perception, narrative shaping, and interactional experience can be detected at least in a rudimentary form in the interaction between patient and therapist. If the patient is unable to establish a structured link with important reference persons and if on the therapist's part there is no possibility of graphically structured interactional experience, then other psychotherapeutic techniques will need to take the foreground. In this respect, a hermeneutic form of perception is also a special diagnostic instrument. If after, say, five sessions of tentative therapy, none of the principles discussed can be implemented, then the probability is high that we are in the presence of disorders that cannot be remedied by activating graphic or scenic fantasy processes. We will then need to resort to long-term psychoanalytic treatment with patient work on resistance and careful, long-term containment of destructive affects and fantasies. Alternatively, we may need to probe whether the patient might respond more favourably to cognitive behavioural therapy or other kinds of intervention. But even if other techniques are employed, the therapist should retain his creative hermeneutic stance.

Counter-indications and limitations to the creative attitude

Psychotic disorders

In dealing with patients with schizophrenic disorders or with paranoid borderline patients, a creative attitude is appropriate, although hermeneutic intervention strategies are not usually effective. The concretistic attitude to symbols and a therapeutic relationship coloured by fear and mistrust normally precludes working with freely engendered ideas and imaginings. In disorders of this kind, psychotherapeutic care will normally concentrate on reality and have a clarifying and structuring function. In certain cases, however, the framework of a course of treatment based on medication or social psychiatry may make it possible to establish psychotherapeutic ground where work on fantasies—in the "as if" of therapeutic language games—may be feasible. In such cases, the therapist will need to take a more active part in providing symbolizations based on structuring fantasies than is the case with neurotic patients (Arieti, 1974; Holm-Hadulla, 1988).

Affective disorders

In severe affective disorders, notably those referred to in earlier European psychiatry as "endogenous", psychotherapeutic care following treatment with medication will again be largely structuring and supportive. Outside the acute phases of depression, the development of coping strategies will have priority. Here the hermeneutic actualization of conflicts and the exploration of resources can be of major significance. The opportunity for creative therapy strategies will depend on the personality structure and the symbolization potential of the depressive patient. On no account should concretistically restricted patients be therapeutically overtaxed in their potential for narrative shaping. In the sector of affective disorders, a differential indication of psychotherapeutic measures geared to different kinds of disorder and the personality of the patient is of major importance.

Somatoform disorders

Here again, dynamic psychotherapy with creative intervention strategies alone is rarely possible because of the patients' restricted scope for fantasies and linguistic symbols. In disorders of this kind, the therapeutic space is not flooded with affects, anxieties, and suspicion as in the case of psychotic patients. Instead, this space is empty and unstructured. Patients and therapists will frequently find it impossible to give a representational structure to signifi-cant images and ideas in the course of interactional experience. In somatization disorders, the kind of approach most likely to work is a combination of body-orientated psychotherapy, art and music therapy, milieu therapy, and interactional individual and group therapy.

Other psychic disorders

Even in the case of the indications for creative dynamic psychother-apy set out above, hermeneutic strategies will need to be supple-mented if patient and therapist fail in the first few sessions to develop fantasies and establish "transitional" therapeutic ground, even if only briefly. If patients with adjustment, anxiety, affective, eating, and personality disorders do not succeed within a relatively short space of time in drawing upon their symbolizing functions for the integration and development of their internal lives, then longer-term psychoanalytic therapy is recommended. This is probably still the best method of assisting patients whose creative potential has taken a chronically pathological turn as a result of suppression and splitting-off. It can help them to discover their resources by way of memory, narrative shaping, and interactional experience. Mean-while there is a degree of empirical evidence substantiating this clinical experience (Crits-Christoph & Barber, 2000, Leuzinger-Bohleber, *et al.*, 2001).

I shall now indicate the counter-indications and limitations of the creative hermeneutic approach with reference to two case histories.

Psychotherapeutic treatment at the onset of schizophrenia

Brigitte, a nineteen-year-old student, arrives at the psychotherapeutic counsel centre after wandering around for an hour without finding the building, although the location had been minutely described to her on the phone by the secretary. In the initial interview, she makes an anxious and disturbed impression on the psychologist she talks to. She appears disorientated, suffering, "altogether a pale, delicate kind of girl, thin, lost and fragile". After a while, Brigitte expresses the fear that someone might be listening in on the interview and starts fearing the therapist's eyes. This fear of the therapist's gaze becomes so delusional that the therapist recommends an interview with a psychiatrist. In the interview with me, Brigitte makes a disturbed, uncertain impression, her movements are abrupt and at first she has difficulty sustaining eye contact. In the intervals she first crumples, then gets restless, looks around disconcertedly. This suggests to me the possibility of a schizo-phrenic condition. When addressed or asked direct questions, however, she takes on more contour, is able to give clear, coherent answers and first-degree schizophrenic symptoms as described by Kurt Schneider are not detectable.

Asked about her complaints, Brigitte says she is unable to learn, study, and concentrate. She says that she is constantly asking herself questions of a fundamental nature, notably whether she is "all right". She describes her own biography in a fragmentary manner, with a strange and mysterious banality. "When I was little I couldn't do up my shoes, and then someone said I must have an early brain trauma." Although her graduation grades were excellent, she still felt that she could not think properly. She was always trying to get to the bottom of things. For example, when the blanket on her bed slipped to the ground, she felt compelled to express this movement in a mathematical formula. Generally speaking, she felt cut off from everything "including myself. Like when nothing goes through your spine. Even now, I'm so con-fused, I have no view of things, my thoughts revolve around them-selves, run away, disappear, come back . . ."

Brigitte's descriptions are conspicuous for their lack of orientation and a marked feeling of being "lost". Once I realize this, I change from a reticent, receptive, sympathetic, observing attitude to a more structur-ing and clarifying approach. Avoiding lengthy pauses in the exchange, which obviously alarm the patient, I get her to discuss her concrete life situation more clearly and in greater detail and depth. She accepts suggestions about her present, real way of life reflectively. We talk about how important it is to get an adequate amount of physical exer-cise and relaxation in times of intellectual strain. She tells me that she enjoyed jazz-dancing but felt that she must give up this activity in order to concentrate on her studies and not to be diverted from her purpose. When I say that such activities are necessary she appears relieved. Discussing her work plan to ensure an adequate, clear-cut distinction between work and leisure time appears important to her. She is surprised that I take an interest in her painting, in which she says she finds her way back to herself.

At the end of the interview, Brigitte has more contour and gratefully accepts my offer to come back in two days' time for a more in-depth exchange. This offer results from my concern that a schizophrenic symptomatology might take shape, making medication unavoidable.

At the second interview, Brigitte seems surer of herself, more outgoing. She reports that she has kept to the schedule I gave her and has been better able to understand her mathematics problems. Long walks have helped to alleviate her insomnia. In general, she finds it easier to concentrate. Brigitte is grateful for my readiness to talk through the detailed course of her day with her: work plan, intervals for rest, leisure-time activities. Gradually I give the interview an anamnestic slant, and it becomes clear that the patient grew up in a very sheltered but emotionally frigid milieu. Her mother was very timorous and hard to pin down, while her father hardly ever put in an appearance. This fragile, uncertain milieu meant that contacts outside the family were anxiously avoided. When she first went to nursery school, she cried all the time. In fact, her mother says that at the time she was always in tears. A similarly incisive juncture was her high-school entry. Here she was completely unable to acclimatize and had to be taken out of school. At the age of 13–14, a spinal deformity made her wear a corset: "I could only do that by switching off my body entirely, I had to play dead." These two years, she says, are like a gap in her biography. First she was still a child, and when she woke up she was an adult. She tells me that she had gaps of this kind in her attitude to her own body at earlier junctures too, but is unable to describe these periods in more detail. She still feels that her body is alien to her; contact with men is entirely unthinkable. In puberty she often entertained thoughts of suicide.

The picture that emerges is that of an extremely timid personality. Brigitte responds with extreme sensitivity to changes in her accustomed surroundings. The sheltered atmosphere at home and in school largely spared her any independent structuring efforts. However, a serious intentionality disorder made itself felt in childhood whenever the patient was faced with new stages in her development. Brigitte was unable to develop personal and consistent objectives, and remained dependent on instructions from the outside. When these instructions are absent or not clear enough, the patient completely loses what is at the best of times a rudimentary and fragile feeling of wholeness. The present crisis has made her lose touch with herself entirely. Boundary loss sets in. The new stage of her life as a student has destabilized the fragile hierarchies of habit, and the patient is helplessly exposed to her own vulnerability. She has insufficient resources for coping with this.

Accordingly, the therapeutic strategy has to attempt to give the patient real structure, provide her actively with meaningful aims, and thus bolster her security. At the same time, it is necessary to identify and activate the coping mechanisms she has at her disposal. In psychodynamic terms, the therapist takes over the role of an auxiliary ego.

> At the third interview, Brigitte manages to recognize that her constant mathematical broodings are a way of phasing out acceptance of the fact that deep down she had set her sights on a different course of study. This is nothing other than the rationalization of her desire to study in and with the protection of her parents' home. Now that she has been accepted for a different course, she feels safely back "on course", and is happy that she can live in her home town, "protected for a while by my parents". One week later she informs me by phone that she has settled in well at home. She expresses the conviction that without the exchanges with me she would have been plunged into a "disaster".

Whether or not the patient would really have encountered a disaster without these structure-giving interviews is something we cannot decide. There is no way of telling from the preliminary stages whether schizophrenic psychosis will in fact develop or not. Only in retrospect, after the full schizophrenic symptomatology has manifested itself, can we identify with certainty the anxieties, the feelings of threat, and the delusive modes of experience as prodromal symptoms of a schizotypic or schizophrenic disorder. But I do believe that in individual cases structure-giving psychotherapeutic counselling can prevent a drift into psychosis. Even if this were only a delay, it would still be valuable, knowing as we do that the prognosis for a psychotic disorder depends on the level of structure achieved by the primary personality. Perhaps the patient will find an opportunity for maturation in the reassuring atmosphere of her parents' home. One might, of course, object that in this sheltered atmosphere the autonomy and separation problem the patient obviously has will be deprived of a working-through. But this would be to ignore the fact that the patient's contact disorder also represents a protection from psychotic disintegration, and thus fulfils an important defence function. In my view, the price to be paid for focusing on the separation problem at the expense of the social network that the patient could only find in her parents' home would have been irresponsibly high, because it would have incurred the danger of further disintegration. Concentration on the separation issue might be congruent with the attitude of the counsellor or therapist, but it would also neglect the patient's vulnerability. One thing we learn from this case is the importance of sound psychological and psychiatric knowledge for psychotherapeutic counselling as a professional activity. If, for example, the therapist generated a silent interview atmosphere with a view to allowing unconscious fantasms to manifest themselves, or if he were to content himself with simple empathy, the patient would be in grave danger of disintegrating altogether. Perceiving this danger, and given his psychiatric experience with patients in a delusive state, the therapist has no choice but to opt for a structure-giving, reality-oriented strategy. I think it important to stress here that the psychiatric and psychodynamic understanding of disintegrative states is precisely the reason for not selecting a psychodynamic or creative/hermeneutic approach in this instance. The strategies of choice in this case are cognitive and behaviour-orientated. Once the corresponding symptoms have developed, these strategies will then support medication treatment.

In longer-term therapies, however, it is possible to employ a cautious hermeneutic approach to achieve an integrating effect on the internal world of a psychotic patient. Accordingly, after the crisis had receded, I recommended to Brigitte a combination of cognitive, behaviour-orientated, and psychodynamic therapy. This reticence *vis-à-vis* both a purely hermeneutic approach and a purely scientific and technical approach in the treatment of schizophrenic disorders will remind those acquainted with the issue of the old difference between understanding and explaining. For more detail on the hermeneutic aspect in psychiatric theory formation and psychotherapy the reader is referred to the very cogent article by Philipps (1996).

Psychotherapy for major depressive disorders

The twenty-eight-year-old medical student, Charles, is about to take his final exams. He reports that for six to eight weeks he has been "losing the ground under his feet". He consulted his family doctor because of his insomnia, and the doctor prescribed sleeping pills and a tranquillizer. His doctoral dissertation causes him particular problems. He has the feeling that what he has assembled so far is an uncoordinated rag-bag. He is seriously contemplating abandoning his studies and becoming a primary school teacher instead. The therapist conducting the initial interview has the impression of low differentiation, with the patient "standing helplessly outside the crisis situation, which he experiences as a personal failure". In her findings she establishes anxiety and depression, coupled with demanding desires for care "stemming from a narcissistic crisis".

The diagnosis identifies an adaptation disorder with mixed emotional features, work difficulties, and a narcissistic personality problem. The therapist discusses the further procedure with Charles, suggesting very strongly that in the present crisis he should not make any important decisions in connection with abandoning his studies. She contemplates offering the patient a number of supportive, structure-enhancing interviews and a place in a work-problems group receiving cognitive, behaviour-orientated therapy.

At the second interview, Charles reports that he has successfully forced himself to engage in the activities recommended by the therapist. But at the weekend he went back home to his parents. The therapist interprets this as a regressive actualization of strong desires for care. Parallel to this consultation, the patient's parents have applied to a marriage and life counselling centre, where Charles' autonomy and separation problem is also regarded as being of crucial importance. The patient and his parents have been recommended to pare down their contact with one another and to attempt to achieve a more well-defined separation.

At the back-up interview one week later, Charles is obviously at pains to adapt to the situation. He reports on his problems with his dissertation. His fear of being totally unsuitable for his medical studies, despite good grades in the exams he has taken so far, has meanwhile turned into a firm conviction. As Charles tells me about the atmosphere at home, his girl-friend, and the way he conducts his everyday life, he appears superficially outgoing, earnestly concerned to report something of essential moment, but emotionally very distant. As I listen, I ask myself why no personal associations or images occur to me in connection with this patient. In the further course of events, the exchange between us remains oddly amorphous, with the patient talking about himself as if he were discussing an engine that is not running smoothly.

After a while, I feel that I have fully plumbed the absence of contour and the vacant nature of the patient's intentionality. Emotionally, despite my invitation to engage with his desires and his fantasy world, Charles remains equally distant both from himself and from me. Accordingly, I decide to use more direct questions in order to get a picture of what the patient's life-world looks like. In contrast to the intangibility of his reaction to inquiries about his desires and fantasies, the patient responds with extreme clarity to concrete questions about the way he leads his life. He tells me that he comes from a very minutely organized and "very, very orderly" civil service background. The worst thing about his present state, he says, is that he is falling behind his fellow students, unable to keep up with their development, and equally unable to fulfil the plan he has conceived for his own progress in life. This inability to stick to a time-plan repeatedly involves fruitless brooding that he finds insupportable. "Falling out of step with his plans" is something that he must spare his parents at all costs. He says that when he takes a closer look at his own self, everything appears "congealed" and "paralysed". He is unable to concentrate and feels as if "everything has been deleted from my brain." In the past he has frequently felt dejected in the winter months, but it has never been so bad before and he has always managed to snap out of it. In the late winter months he used to imagine the colours of spring and this gave him almost a feeling of happiness. But now everything is grey, and it looks as if it is going to stay that way.

After this account, the diagnosis that suggests itself to me is that of a major depressive disorder. Accordingly, I relinquish the scenic, interactive level of communication. My perplexity begins to recede, and in the course of my further observations the patient presents a typically melancholic condition with amorphous mood impairment, lack of impetus, daytime fluctuations with morning "lows", dyssomnia, and other impairments of his general vitality. It also becomes apparent that in the last few weeks the patient has not only toyed with thoughts of suicide but has experienced them in an increasingly urgent form.

On the other hand, the patient's mood impairment is not so marked that he can no longer cope with the normal conduct of his

life. This is probably what prompted the first therapist who exam-
ined him to conclude that the depression was "not all that severe".
There are many patients with neurotically depressive disorders
who give the impression of being much more severely ill. But the
diagnosis does seem fairly well grounded. Basing a differential
diagnosis of neurotic or "endogenous" depression (this approach is
still of major significance in European psychiatry) wholly on the
severity of the depressive mood impairment complained of by the
patient can lead to serious errors.

> Talking over further moves with Charles, the first thing I attempt to do
> is to take the strain off him. He is relieved when I tell him that he is in
> a state of profound crisis and serious illness, for which he himself is not
> responsible. First I prescribe the antidepressant amitryptilin in increas-
> ing dosages, and offer him a close-knit care regime. Although the
> patient is grateful for the offer of regular interviews, there is little
> change in the first two or three weeks. Charles remains monothematic,
> despairing, and there is no alleviation of his complaints. However, he
> is punctilious in attending the two sessions a week offered him, and
> later, when the complaints have receded, he remarks that these regular
> appointments "held him in place." After four weeks of treatment and
> the additional administration of clomipramin, there is still no major
> improvement in his condition, and I am grateful for confirmation of my
> diagnosis by a neurologist examining Charles to rule out organic
> causes. After another two weeks of medication with amitryptilin and
> fluoxetin, there is a substantial improvement. The patient makes a more
> flexible impression, he has been reading one or two books required for
> his exams, and says that he has been able to memorize some of the
> content. Two weeks later he has resumed his exam preparations, is
> working solidly, spends the evenings with his girl-friend, and is
> described by her as consistently cheerful, "like he used to be". His
> parents, who had come for a joint session at the beginning of treatment,
> are very gratified at the turn things have taken, and tell me that they
> could hardly have imagined such a change to be possible. They also
> tell me that one of Charles' uncles suffered from recurrent depress-
> ive episodes and that another relative committed suicide in a fit of
> depression.

After the clinical symptoms have faded, Charles wants to
continue the psychotherapeutic interviews on a once-a-week basis,
first because he fears that the phase he has been through might

repeat itself, second, to work on ways of protecting himself from such a recurrence in future, and third, to clarify a number of "diffuse" conflicts. In a total of twenty-five psychotherapeutic sessions we work on his feelings of guilt associated with the discovery of his independence and his own desires. Whenever he experiences expansive impulses, the immediate upshot is the feeling that he is abandoning his parents and also jeopardizing the emotional balance between himself and his girl-friend. It becomes apparent that for years the patient has been denying libidinous, expansive desires. In our exchanges he succeeds in establishing a relationship to his desires, although they do not fit in with the role-image he has established for himself. Whether the increase in flexibility and inner freedom achieved in the course of the psychotherapeutic sessions can protect Charles from a relapse into a depressive phase is a question that cannot be answered. But at all events, these sessions have certainly established a relationship of trust, and it seems likely that, if such a depressive phase recurs, then the patient will apply for professional aid in overcoming it. He will then be given expert assistance at a much earlier stage, and this in its turn will lower the substantial risks involved in bouts of depression.

In Charles' case it became apparent in the initial sessions that he could not be helped with hermeneutic principles and intervention strategies and that a different course of treatment was indicated. Like patients with severe psychosomatic disorders and schizophrenic disturbances, patients suffering from endogenous depression do not respond to therapy based on memory, narrative shaping, and interactional experience. Here the therapist and/or the therapeutic team must draw upon the entire range of cognitive, behaviour-orientated, psychodynamic and medicational treatment forms available to them.

Concluding remarks on indications and counter-indications

Summing up the indication and counter-indication of creative counselling, we can say that essentially the intervention strategies involved are aimed at the solution of present conflicts. Creative psychodynamic psychotherapy goes further. Here psychogenic symptoms are "replaced" by memory, narrative shaping, and interactional experience. While profound disorders cannot be dealt within brief psychotherapy, it is possible to initiate a constructive approach to them. Also, counselling or brief psychotherapy can be a preparation for longer-term psychotherapeutic treatment. From the cases we have discussed it has become apparent that counselling and brief creative psychotherapy cannot provide a "working through" of elemental conflicts. But it can instil a way of dealing with conflicts that the patient can develop further after therapy. The representation of internal and external reality can bring about a more acute perception of personal resources and with it a more satisfactory relationship with the patient's life-world.

The essential factor determining the prognosis for creative counselling and psychotherapy is the establishment of productive interaction between counsellor and client, patient and therapist. The helping alliance will be useful in creative counselling and psychotherapy if it enables the patient to develop fantasies, graphic ideas, and memories. The counsellor/therapist must also be able, if only briefly, to create an undisturbed space in which he can follow up these images in his own inner world. Another determining factor for the prognosis is the question of whether these images serve to extend perceptual competence and a better understanding of the client's or patient's own reality, thus also indicating possibilities for action. If, as in the first of the case histories we looked at, a positive interaction is swiftly established, then the prognosis will be favourable even in the presence of pronounced symptoms.

I consider the indication and prognosis criteria to be empirical in the original sense of the word. However, I am also fully alive to the fact that their subjective nature makes them susceptible to error, notably if they are applied by inexperienced counsellors and psychotherapists. In clinical routine it is thus of crucial importance to present one's views for assessment in the framework of case discussions and supervision. In this way they can be validated in an exchange with colleagues on the basis of reflection from the viewpoint of other experts.

Apart from differences in indication, counselling and therapy also differ in their objectives. Creative counselling is geared to the removal and solution of present problems and conflict situations. Creative dynamic psychotherapy on a hermeneutic basis serves to alleviate more deep-seated psychic disorders. The two approaches overlap notably in crisis intervention. In formal terms it has proved a good idea to limit creative counselling to ten double sessions and brief dynamic psychotherapy to twenty-five sessions. But hermeneutic principles are also effective in many long-term psychodynamic treatment forms, above all in psychoanalysis.

CHAPTER ELEVEN

Professional and "ordinary" relationships

The clients and patients described in our counselling and therapy accounts want nothing more than to be "at home" in their internal and external worlds. All of us need to establish a place for ourselves in our life-worlds. This process takes place in our work, in the creation of a private sphere, and in our partnerships. Even in a fulfilled and fulfilling love relationship we are constantly faced with the task of giving it a meaningful structure and maintaining that structure. In this, there is no difference between ordinary couple relationships and the therapeutic variety. While patient and therapist are certainly a special kind of couple, they too, like other couples, must take an active part in giving their relationship meaning and structure. A relationship with another person involves a never-ending creative process. In that process we become acquainted not only with the other person involved but also with the otherness of our own selves and the otherness of our partner(s). This acquaintance requires a presentational and symbolic form, and it requires us to give it that form. This goes well beyond the factual identification or discovery of the "way we (or other persons) are". Partners who mutually establish their "factual" selves once and for all are depriving themselves of the opportunity for joint development.

There are, however, many obstacles to development in partnership, including the need for stability, security, definition. The creative development of our emotional lives and our capacity for fantasy may be experienced as something unsettling, not to say dangerous. But there are many couples who discover how inspiring it can be to constantly discover each other anew. It may be that we do not have the necessary range of psychological concepts to put a name to this experience. For this reason, I return here to the hermeneutic conception of conversation, noting as I do so that every conversation between partners takes place against the (frequently unconscious) backdrop of a world of pictorial and scenic images.

> We say that we "conduct" a conversation, but the more genuine a conversation is, the less its conduct lies within the will of either partner. Thus a genuine conversation is never the one that we wanted to conduct. Rather, it is more generally correct to say that we fall into a conversation, or even that we become involved in it. [. . .] No one knows in advance what will "come out" of a conversation." [Gadamer, 1960, p. 383]

Thus, if a partnership is to succeed it requires us to be open for new things and sensitive to the unconscious; in short to be receptive to

> What, unknown to many
> Or even derided,
> Through the mazes of the breast
> Wanders in the night.
>   [Goethe, 'To the Moon']

To this extent we can say that the fact that love makes us blind is not merely a reference to a deception that will stand revealed by everyday reality at some point, it is also a permanent opportunity to see the loved one differently. At the same time, this blindness is an opportunity to discover different and new aspects of our own selves, and thus to experience our existence in the partnership as a development.

Let me put this in more concrete terms. For couples it may be a significant experience to gain access to sexual fantasies within their relationship that have remained unconscious for a long time and have had insidious, detrimental effects in the conflicts taking place in that relationship. Normally, contact with the fantasies of love-partners is unconscious. But it can be important and trust-building for this to happen at a conscious level. When the partners are able to relate to these fantasies, although they may appear strange or alarming, they will derive encouragement from this for the development of their fantasy games. In this way a successful partnership can be progressively enriched by new aspects that guarantee the vitality of the couple's relationship. Frequently, couples shy away from such a development because it may seem to militate against stability and security. But the price for this kind of security, achieved by withdrawal from precarious inner processes, is high. It consists in mistrust, jealousy, feelings and moods of resentment that undermine the couple's relationship. A partnership that lives on the unchanging, controlled reliability of the partner will usually end up at an impasse. A couple will be happy to the extent that the two partners succeed in accepting, appreciating, and enjoying each other's feelings and fantasies as a game they can both share in.

Naturally, a development of this kind requires time and care. As in psychotherapy, the articulation of moods and obscure fantasies in a couple relationship call for tact and timing, and require an active appreciation of the other's inner vitality, even though it can impose strains on the need for security and familiarity. However, the reward of this occasional discomfiture in the form of heightened vitality is higher than the price exacted by a loss of security.

Earlier, I quoted Winnicott as saying that a therapeutic relationship is productive when patient and therapist succeed in "playing with one another". But this game should not stand in contrast to reality, it should lead to new perspectives and ultimately to a constructive approach to that reality. To this extent, every successful partnership has an element of the artistic about it. The art of sustaining a partnership is essentially constituted by a constellation in which the imaginatively structured internal development of one partner encourages the forces structuring the internal development of the other.

In our case histories we saw how important it is for patient and therapist to develop an ear for the language, the sorrow or the happiness of the child within, to experience the glooms and jubilations of adolescence, and to appreciate the security afforded by the more circumspect and limiting attitudes of adults. At the same time, it will be essential for them to welcome, or at least tolerate, these aspects in their partners. They must assume a kind of stewardship for the child within, both within themselves and within the partner, and relate these elements to one another.

In creative counselling and psychotherapy, the "professional" couple assumes the stewardship for unstructured, threatening, sometimes even repulsive or rejected elements that I have subsumed in the term "the child within". Earlier phases of our development are not simply stages that we have overcome and left behind. The child within us, with all its hope and anxieties, is a permanent companion throughout our lives. Its covert actuality is not, however, an "anachronistic" source of anxieties and perturbations, it is an imaginative and hopeful part of ourselves, and as such a significant resource that we can draw on in our adult lives. The anachronistic sides of our partners are also something we should accept and learn to appreciate. The adolescent within is not only threatening because of the chaotically unstructured nature of his/ her drive impulses, but is also vital and full of a potential for discovery. With their experience, far-sightedness, and common sense, adults can give the child and the adolescent a framework within which they can live this game out to the full. An essential aspect of the "art of relationships", I would say, is for the partners to integrate different internal objects and configurations of self into a tolerant, rather than a hostile or marginalizing form of communication.

Fortunately, there is a corrective for the more confusing aspects of a therapeutic couple relationship. It is the therapeutic and professional attitude. Together with our theoretical and technical knowledge of the way to approach treatment, it is an important resource to draw upon when free exchange threatens to break down and for dealing with the difficulties that then necessarily ensue. It is an attitude characterized not by dogmatism and text-book principles but gained from the experiences gleaned by our predecessors, experiences that it is our job to integrate and enlarge upon. One such experience is the concept of therapeutic ego-splitting, which implies the dialectic of, and between, an empathic, sympathetic attitude and observation and critical scrutiny. Even in periods when the joint development with our patients is interesting and productive, this dual attitude acts as a guard against that development turning into too close an involvement.

This is the explanation for the apparently paradoxical insight that it takes a clinically experienced therapist, an expert well versed in the entire range of possible psychic disorders, to be able to enter into an interactional game with the patient that is free of theoretically grounded constraints. Free play of this nature requires an established ground if it is to thrive. Part of that ground is provided by the therapist's capacity for clinical reflection. This capacity is the root of his neutrality and his receptiveness for the patient. However, it is not the sole component of the ground on which we stand. A further element is the knowledge of the presentation of human conflicts to be found in mythology, cultural history, and literature. A third constituent of therapeutic treatment to which I have given especial attention is the ability to play with the fantasies that patients set off in us. It is here that we are confronted with our own contradictions; contradictions that we are called upon not to resolve but, initially at least, to accept as part of our psychic existence.

In extra-therapeutic couple relationships we also find something similar to a therapeutic ego-splitting, a separation into an existential, intuitively empathic attitude, and the "expert" approach born of knowledge and rational judgment. We are acquainted both with the world of the profound, intense, and pre-conscious experience of the "heady confusion" caused by passion, and with that of conscious, clear-headed cultivation of morality and life-style that is not merely drab and "ordinary" (just as the theory on which a psychotherapist bases his approach is not drab or uniform) but guarantees reliability, constancy, continuity, and the familiarity of "home ground".

The emotional interchange between the couple can be captured more completely with the concept of *projective identification*. As we have seen, partners in couple relationships assist each other in the perception of initially inaccessible feelings and modes of experience. This happens because the partners not only understand one another on an intellectual plane but take a vital and active living interest in one another. This sharing of experience is essentially a matter of projective identification. The meaning of this term can perhaps best be summarized as a process in which one partner generates ideas and modes of experience in the other, while at the same time staying "in touch" with them. The relationship will succeed if the other partner can relate to this projection, connect it with his or her own subjective experience of things, and thus make contact with the subjective experience of the first partner. Here, there are significant differences between therapeutic and "ordinary" couple relationships. In a therapeutic relationship, it devolves upon the therapist to take up what the patient communicates in his or her projections—affects, ideas, unintegrated modes of experience—and to work on them and structure them *for* the patient. In contrast to ordinary couple relationships, the patient has the right and the freedom to "exploit" the therapist as a projection surface for his or her fantasies and emotional needs. For her part, it is incumbent upon the therapist to use her own fantasies in a controlled manner to enhance her understanding of the patient. Then, if all goes well, the patient's fragmented and inadequately structured subjective experience will gel into a meaningful structure. If this process succeeds, and the therapist's capacity for linguistic and graphic structuring is adequate to the task, the patient will be able to make contact with aspects of his or her internal life that have so far evaded perception and subjective experience, and to accept these elements into his or her psychic ambience. In non-therapeutic relationships, this mutual process develops in a less one-sided way. Partners in ordinary relationships play with one another more directly and immediately. But here too, both partners must have sufficient scope to maintain a degree of independence in the conduct of their own internal games.

Clients and patients provide access to a counselling or therapeutic "play area" by virtue of the very fact that they agree to speak. As we have seen, they provide more than mere information from which the counsellor or therapist can draw correct conclusions or derive accurate explanations. By way of metaphors, scenes, dreams, and graphic stories, they invite her to accompany them into their own world. The counsellor or therapist can only follow by "playing along," empathizing with, say, the childlike worries and troubles of the client or patient, or achieving an emotional understanding of the feelings and concerns of the parents in their interactions with the client or patient. Only by constantly confronting and relating to this internal development will she be able to understand the client or patient in the hermeneutic, deep-psychological sense of the term. The essential point is the acceptance of this stewardship for the otherness we find both in ourselves and in others.

Clients seeking counselling, patients, couples, and we ourselves in our everyday existence, are constantly faced with disturbances in the development process. Again and again we have to mobilize our psychic faculties to evade being drawn into apathy and dejection. In representing this view, I am in accord with Freud's dualist drive theory that situates human development in the duality of the life and death drives, love and hatred, *eros* and *thanatos*. It is this task of continuing development that we must accept. As Goethe says at the end of "Blissful Yearning":

> And as long as you don't attain it,
> This "die and become!"
> You will be a doleful guest
> On this dark earth.

In this sense, life is a creative process of suffering. If we can accept this view, instead of indulging in more comfortable but ultimately regressive and destructive habits, then we will attain genuine development and the new joys that go with it.

The development process imposed upon us anthropologically can be understood as a creative activity. This means first of all work, in the narrower sense of giving shape to the external world; on the other hand, it implies imposing a structure on our inner relations with our fellow humans, our own selves, and our affects (see Kernberg, 1980). This process never comes to an end. Any attempt to evade the necessity of constant shaping and structuring, sustained perhaps by the desire for tension-free sameness and for things to "stay as they are", will lead to a state of terminal equanimity that involves a hazardous dialectic. Personal relationships become empty, destructive urges assert themselves and are processed projectively, leading to a state best described as a vicious circle. Thus, we must insist once again that true partnership only exists in the form of structuring development.

CHAPTER TWELVE

Ethical implications

As in medicine generally, the last few years have also seen an increasing concern with ethical issues in counselling and psychotherapy. A number of ethical consequences can be derived from a hermeneutic stance. In the following, I shall take my bearings from the influential ethical model proposed by Beauchamp & Childress (1989). This model proceeds on four principles:

- non-maleficence
- respect for the patient's autonomy
- beneficence
- justice and equitableness.

Non-maleficence

The first principle (*primum non nocere*) confronts the counsellor or psychotherapist with the question of the extent to which he can expect the client or patient to sustain such things as grief and despair. For very good reasons, many psychotherapists consider it to be a fundamental aspect of psychic health for patients to be able to stand up to feelings of dejection and existential uncertainty, and also to achieve a well-defined emotional perception of the fact that we all have the potential for good and evil in our personalities (Melanie Klein calls this the "depressive position".) It would be naïve to evade this question and declare the whole issue to be a matter of the client's or patient's decision-making competence. It is impossible to enlighten the client or patient from the outset on, say, fantasies that he will only discover to be a part of himself in the course of treatment. At best, the client or patient may have an intuitive conviction that an actualization of unfamiliar ideas and notions will be helpful. In this, all he/she can do is to trust that the counsellor or therapist is a suitable companion in this process of discovery. On this issue, the approach advocated by creative counselling or psychotherapy can be of assistance, as long as no one-sidedly authoritative treatment objective is formulated in the framework of this basic approach. Rather, the principle of scenic interaction results in patients constantly redefining their objectives and only pursuing them to the extent that they follow on from the interaction with the therapist. The counsellor or therapist will not expressly formulate a well-defined concept of adequate behaviour or psychic health (although, of course, he has such a concept for himself and also on the basis of the theories he espouses) but in conjunction with the client or patient will be guided by his or her stages of development.

Respect for the patient's autonomy

Respecting the wishes, objectives, and life goals of others would appear at first glance to be self-evident. At a second glance, however, doubts assert themselves. We do not need to be a psychoanalytic therapist or a professional psychologist to be aware of the fact that in many ways we are hidden from ourselves. Psychoanalysis has attempted to grasp this fact with the help of concepts pertaining to the unconscious impulses invariably active in our psychological lives. And outside specifically psychoanalytic theory there is general acceptance that one of the central reasons for clients or patients to seek help is closely bound up with unconscious or implicit psychic impulses. How, then, can one cast light, at least initially, on something to which the client or patient cannot relate? And do we really know the causes of disorder in each individual case? Counsellors and therapists working on a cognitive behavioural basis avail themselves of learning-theory models to explain to clients and patients the grounds for their disturbance. But in most cases research has not advanced far enough to decide which factors—genetic, learning-theoretic, psychodynamic—are the really essential ones. Accordingly, modesty appears to me to be a central virtue when it comes to explaining psychic disturbances.

Respect for the client's and patient's autonomy as an ethical principle can be fostered by the basic creative attitude and its specific mode of perception. What it does is to attempt to help the client and patient to achieve authentic experience of his or her life-world. Unlike the pure application of counselling or psychotherapeutic techniques, it seeks to open up a space for immediate and subjective perception. This makes it empirical in the original sense of the term.

By contrast, cognitive explanations can further mechanize and "technologize" those elements of a client's or patient's emotional life that he or she has not yet adequately structured and therefore attempts to come to terms with concretistically in the form of distress and symptoms. The upshot of this can be a perpetuation or even an aggravation of suffering and dependency under the guise of strengthening the patient's autonomy.

Beneficence

Occasionally, the obligation to provide help and the principle of care for the client or patient will be at odds with the principle of autonomy. In terms of the Christian ethic, care means taking on responsibility for the welfare of the client or patient. In counselling and psychotherapy, this is a problem of a very special kind. The creative approach appears to me to suggest a way of reconciling the principles of care and autonomy. As long as we are guided by the client's and patient's development and potential for development, then both these principles can be respected in equal measure. For example, if we act in accordance with the principle of receptiveness for the client's or patient's world of subjective experience, then this will involve both respect for the client's and patient's autonomy and a caring attitude towards him or her. This does not take place automatically, however, but has to be constantly fought for and subjected to a checking and testing process, both with the patient and in the expert community. Accordingly, part of the obligation that care of the client or patient imposes on us is to seek advice from other colleagues when the counselling or psychotherapeutic process runs into trouble. A mechanized evaluation system cannot be a substitute for the validation provided by supervision and inter-vision, because here we are dealing with communicative processes that cannot be captured by objectifying instruments. In this sense, permanent reflection on one's own views with the help of feedback from the expert community is an indispensable part of the obliga-tion to act in a "beneficent" manner.

Justice and equitableness

The principle of equitableness is again one that appears self-evident. But here, too, we quickly encounter problems. Clients and patients are not the same, and there is adequate empirical evidence to substantiate the clinical realization that different clients and patients profit to a different extent from different therapeutic proce-dures. Counsellors and therapists themselves also differ, of course, and are able to work better with one method and one group of clients or patients than another. But it is important to have know-ledge of other methods and of clients or patients who are not ideally suited to the methods we happen to prefer. The creative approach lives on difference. Only by contact with "otherness" can we learn to understand. The same is true of differing counselling and therapeutic approaches. Gadamer speaks of the hermeneutic function of "distance" (see p. 33, above). In my view it is essential for counsellors and therapists to find out in the course of their education what methods and what clients and patients they can work best with. "Easy" clients and patients are, to my mind, a myth. Experienced counsellors and therapists all know of the immense problems that can crop up in the treatment of the so-called *yavis* (young-attractive-verbal-intelligent-sophisticated) and the profound satisfaction that can be derived from the stabilization of an underprivileged patient with a polysymptomatic neurosis and a personality disorder. Here again, the creative approach can help in using different treatment procedures and matching them to different cases.

The four principles of Beauchamp & Childress (1989) can only be a very rough guide to the ethical problems encountered in counselling and psychotherapy. They can never replace judgmental criteria. Training in the creative approach appears to me to hold out better prospects for filling these principles with living content. This professional creative approach is first of all a form of counselling and psychotherapeutic *practice* based on a validation achieved by a consensus with colleagues and the clients and patients. Practice means an art of counselling or therapy based on reflection, *applicatio* in the sense in which Gadamer's practical philosophy uses it. It stands in diametrical opposition to the deductive derivation of maxims for action from principles. I shall now illustrate this point in connection with issues revolving around the counselling or therapy contract, the objectives of counselling and therapy, and the counselling and therapeutic relationship.

Therapy contract, problem definition, objectives, and therapeutic relationship

On the basis of the creative attitude, clients and counsellors, patients and therapists jointly elaborate the counselling or therapy contract, the problem definition, and the objectives of counselling or therapy. There is no way of determining the problem and the conflict situation beforehand; this will emerge in stages from the dialogic encounter. Thus, there is little sense in making lengthy theoretical statements from the outset about the course of counselling or treatment and the objectives it aims at. They would overtax the client or patient and also demand from him or her decisions that cannot be subjectively meaningful at this stage. Long preliminary explanations would inhibit the client's or patient's personal development. This, of course, does not extend to information for the client or patient on the aims and the risks of treatment. But the counsellor or therapist can only grant the client or patient the necessary scope for free decisions if she knows the potentialities and limitations of different counselling and psychotherapeutic procedures and—as required by creative psychotherapy—possesses sufficient inner free-dom and receptiveness for the client's or patient's concerns to be able to accompany him or her on the itinerary ahead. This kind of scope can hardly be replaced by technical rules, but it has to be subject to the control provided by supervision and intervision.

Even more difficult to define is the ideal "fit" between client and counsellor, patient and therapist. This is a matter not only of personality-related sympathies and antipathies but also of multi-faceted unconscious interactions. It is by no means always the case that a client–counsellor or patient–therapist couple with a high degree of sympathy will achieve better results in treatment. Indeed, an initial antipathy can sometimes provide a valuable impetus for personal development, both on the part of the client or patient and of the counsellor or therapist. Here "informed consent" is a particu-larly difficult issue, and the solution needs to be sought not in moral maxims but again in a validation of practical counselling psychotherapeutic action on the basis of consensus and communi-cation.

Development as an objective and an ethical guideline

Even without a clearly framed definition of objectives, the hermen-eutic concept of development can play a guiding role in accom-panying the client or patient on his progress out of distress, a psychic crisis, or illness. This concept includes, as a matter of course, the client's or patient's life-world, meaning that the devel-opment undergone by his or her life companions must not only be kept in mind but given tangible presence in the transitional space of the professional setting. Then the problem of the protection of the interests of third parties in counselling and psychotherapy is reduced to a purely formal status, as development in the creative sense extends quite naturally to social development and the devel-opment of partnerships.

Incidentally, ethical objections are frequently more common in connection with long-term therapies, as if, due to their personal and scientific convictions, psychoanalysts were notorious for involving their patients in over-long courses of treatment. Today, I have the impression that fear of the psychodynamic work demanded by patients and intimidation in the face of public criticism has tended to prompt therapists to favour the kind of distance afforded by technological therapies. And yet, if there is one thing we know, it is that the successful development of a good therapeutic relationship takes time. To some extent, "oblivion" with regard to time can be an important element in therapy. It gives us the opportunity to correct a purely technological attitude to ourselves and others, and to discover the subjectivity that we and others have. Given this fact, it would be a misconceived form of pragmatism to restrict oneself to as swift a reduction of symptoms as possible and to neglect the personal development that has given those symptoms their persistence. Just as a strong attachment to the therapist can be harmful for a patient, so a deliberately "technical" attitude to the patient can also hinder his or her development. In explicitly technical and rational forms of therapy, attachments and emotions are only ostensibly avoided. In reality, they are frequently exploited in a charismatic and unreflecting way. But is such an attitude the right one when patients are keen to discover their emotional world in an atmosphere of trust and long to establish emotional contact with themselves and others by other routes than those provided by the formation of symptoms? Here, in the application of therapeutic techniques, the creative approach can safeguard us against losing sight of the client's and patient's subjectivity and his/her personal potential for development.

The creative approach should also help to prevent us from subjecting clients and patients undergoing counselling or psychotherapy to an ideal of development and health that stems more from the personal views and professional convictions of the counsellor or therapist than from developmental objectives geared to the clients' and patients' own life-world.

This concept of development and the role of narrative shaping in the counselling and therapeutic process also has special consequences for counsellors' and therapists' experience of themselves. From the specific logic of my remarks it should be evident that this does not primarily have to do with the detection of distress and pathological conflicts, but rather with the extension of the internal and external perceptive competence of the counsellor or therapist. Readiness to embark on such a development in communicative encounters should be sufficient protection against self-overestimation and disdain for clients and patients, tricked out in technical and theoretical garb.

The ethics of the creative attitude

The creative attitude implies the insight that there can be no finality in the kind of understanding that promotes development. Each individual is bound to remain mysterious both to himself and others. It is this that produces the specific suspense and excitement of human life. Understanding that encourages authentic development potential goes beyond cognitive rationality and embraces the propensity for physical and psychic involvement. Understanding, thus, becomes an act of transformation. As such it is invariably related to the "other". Gadamer puts this with admirable trenchancy. "The Socratic 'I know that I know nothing' means in practice that the other person might in fact be right" (Gadamer, 1996, p. 10). This conclusion has major social and political repercussions. If hermeneutics means respect for these mysteries and a feeling for the world's wealth of meaning, if it proceeds on the assumption that the other might be right, then in terms of political commitment the implication is that, in contrast to demagogy or advertising psychology, the use of speech is there not to persuade or subjugate the other but to attain to a shared construction of reality. Speech and action, thus understood, mean that we do not merely have things to say and things to do, but that we are also prepared to listen to what others have to say and to respect their actions. This is a fundamental principle of democracy. Understanding takes the place of brute force. The human world is then a community based on communication.

In the age of the electronic media, conversation, understood as the internalizing acceptance of a question posed to us by the matter in hand, by the other person(s) involved in the exchange, and by ourselves, has become difficult. Information penetrates us, and on various occasions remains in our inner selves as a foreign body, as something extraneous. One aim of such information is to evade or prevent any further inquiry, to become (as the psychology of advertising tells us quite openly) an incontrovertible ingredient of our feeling and thinking. The hermeneutic premise for true under-standing, the interweave of question, answer, impression, expres-sion, is precluded. The linguistic nature of genuine exchange is swamped by communication technology. The question then is whether anything approaching solidarity can emerge under such circumstances, at least a species of solidarity that unites us in understanding and mutual respect. Should language in the public sphere end up impoverished in this way, then Gadamer fears that

> the individual will retire into a cave of images and noises. A shadow-world, in which despite the glut of information all is narrow and empty. Information is quick, truths need time. They need time to find their slow way into language. It is art, above all, that addresses all our senses and thus gives us something to under-stand that goes beyond mere information [*ibid.*, p. 12]

In Gadamer's view, the socio-psychological and political signif-icance of art and of the apologia for ordinary language implied once more in this passage should act as a corrective to the unfounded pretension that "the culture of the sciences is the only one that can lay claim to truth" (*ibid.*). In his ninety-sixth year, Gadamer summa-rized his position on this point as follows:

> I would say that it will be a major task for humanity to grasp the limitations of the great heritage of scientific culture. If this fails, then we will certainly end by destroying ourselves. I am not in favour of strictures on science and research, we cannot eliminate the risks involved in misuse. And yet I believe that we must address the danger implicit in the fact that the power invested in human agency is becoming ever stronger, ever larger, and hence ever more likely to end in self-destruction. This is an immense task, always supposing that humankind manages to survive. And it will only manage to do so if the one-sided aspiration to control everything and be able to do everything is offset by the cultivation of other forces, for example, those of suffering and compassion, or, to put it in a poet's words, if we learn to honor the capacity of the human spirit to dream. I believe that this will always depend on the degree of extremity in which we philosophers find our way through life in our indepen-dent questioning and understanding, in our limitations. We shall have to accept all the disappointments with ourselves that we encounter. Nature has prohibited us mightily from learning to

accept death. And yet we must live with the awareness of our mortality and—I hope—resign ourselves to it without mutual extermination. Whether humankind will be able to do that, whether there is anything that can genuinely help us to do so, is a question that I would not venture to answer. [*ibid.*, p. 13]

The question that arises, of course, is whether such existential resignation can release positive forces. This is the great issue addressed by the myth of Prometheus, who boasted that he had freed his fellow humans of the knowledge of the hour of their deaths and thus claimed to be the initiator of the inventive spirit and of the achievements and the energies necessary for humanity to rule the world. "In this sense, I would say that learning to die is equivalent to learning to accept what makes life worth living" (*ibid.*, p. 14).

Seen thus, hermeneutic understanding and acceptance are an integral part of the art of living.

Consequences for the training of counsellors and psychotherapists

From a creative and hermeneutic viewpoint, scientific training can never be adequate in itself. Training in counselling and psychotherapy must instil the ability to apply theoretical knowledge to the individual case. This application is not the straightforward implementation involved in bringing scientific knowledge to bear on a technical process. Rather, it radically changes theoretical knowledge by bringing into play the subjectivity of the client's or patient's and the counsellor's or therapist's mode of experiencing things. This subjectivity is not so much the subject of scientific discipline as of a living engagement with reality, of a kind that we can learn more about from the structures imposed upon it, in a mixture of sensual address and practical achievement, by literature, art, cinema, theatre, music. Accordingly, it is important for budding counsellors and therapists to immerse themselves in the artistic forms of engagement with our life-world, and this not merely as relaxation or recreation. Such earnest inquiry should be an indispensable part of the professional socialization of each and every therapist.

Engagement with our cultural heritage brings with it a receptiveness for different shadings of human existence. However, in itself it is not sufficient to provide the necessary inner freedom and flexibility required to represent the client's or patient's subjective experience adequately in one's own self as a counsellor or therapist. Here, an additional degree of intrepidity is necessary, associated with control of one's feelings of shame and, above all, with creativity. This can be achieved by solidly grounded experience of one's own self. It is true that self-experience of this kind does not always afford the results required for training purposes. But I would certainly not conclude from this that thorough experience of the self should no longer be an integral part of counselling and psychotherapeutic training. On the contrary. I would emphasize that the awareness of one's own self that encourages the capacity for memory, narrative shaping, and interactional experience is an essential resource for counsellors and therapists accompanying clients and patients on the discovery of their existential conflicts. In my view, psychoanalysis is still one of the best media for such creative self-experience.

CHAPTER THIRTEEN

Artistic shaping and resolution of psychic conflicts

I n the following I shall be examining the engagement with psychic conflicts via artistic activity and the structural similarities between the therapeutic and artistic approach to such problems. Ever since its origins in the work of Sigmund Freud, psychoanalysis has repeatedly won decisive insights from the observation of the artistic approach to human conflicts. Notably, literary works have formed the basis for inquiry of this kind. Beginning with Oedipus, psychoanalysts have identified in the great figures of literature central constellations of conflicts and motives that reoccur again and again in the human psyche. Sculpture and the pictorial arts have also been crucial sources of scientific inspiration in this respect. Of especial note is the hermeneutic dialogue that the psychoanalyst Freud engages in with the relevant work of art. Although he does not abstain from providing an analytic interpretation, he does so with the scientific modesty of one who concedes to the artist's mind a very close affinity to the unconscious and to the products of the artistic imagination a definite superiority over the scientific approach: "That which we cannot gain in flight we must achieve with our halting gait." The intention behind this dictum of Freud's is to characterize the slow, fragmentary nature of analytic research over and against the direct, cogent, immediately visual nature of artistic achievement. The artist's capacity for portraying the unconscious in a ludic manner is one reason why Freud frequently insisted that every psychotherapist stands to learn a great deal from the contemplation of art.

As artworks have left their mark on psychoanalysis, so psycho-analysts have applied their analytic techniques to artworks and artists. This has frequently been taken amiss. The controversy has also tended to blind us to the fact that art, counselling, and psycho-therapy can fulfil similar psychic and communicative functions. Counselling, psychotherapy, and art are not only interpretations of things that have happened, they are shaping, structuring processes that give subjective experience a coherent form. I have already indi-cated this in the chapter on psychotherapy as an aesthetic structur-ing process. I now propose to look at three examples of the ways in which psychic crises and conflicts can be coped with by means of artistic creativity. For this purpose I have chosen Goethe, Rilke, and Neruda, largely because of the affinity I feel for these authors. Readers will perhaps be reminded of their own favourite authors and their own experiences.

As a young man, Johann Wolfgang von Goethe left his sheltered home in Frankfurt to study law in Leipzig. In his new surroundings he felt lonely and suffered from home-sickness. His first affections for young ladies were unrequited and these "failures" diverted almost all his attention from his studies. Increasingly he withdrew into himself and developed a number of physical symptoms. Constipation, recurring infections, and a growth on his neck caused him considerable distress, and he also suffered frequent tooth-ache, a persistent cough, a general inability to work, and hypochon-driac fears (Friedenthal, 1963). He consulted a number of doctors in search of medical aid and in retrospect there have also been a whole array of more or less well-substantiated speculations about what it was he actually had. They range from syphilis and tuberculosis to some form of psychogenic disorder. Goethe himself had the feeling that his "brain was darkened and the entrails paralysed". In this period he vacillated between bouts of hectic gaiety and fits of profound distress culminating in suicidal fantasies. On the basis of his written testimonies, one renowned twentieth century psychia-trist diagnosed a manic-depressive disorder, while another was convinced that Goethe was suffering from psychotic episodes (Eissler, 1963). These diagnoses are hardly compatible with clinical psychopathology as we know it today, nor with classical views of psychoses. All that we really have to go on is the certain knowledge that in his early student days Goethe went through a severe crisis, possibly the most severe in his entire life. Although by no means spared a number of similar crises in his later years, he was later to look back on this particular period as one of total and utter misery.

But Goethe was not just any young man. In this period of separation from home, unrequited love, and then the worry caused by severe physical ailments, his innate genius enabled him to come to terms with the various sufferings he went through. His creative abilities showed him the way out of his profound psychological distress and enlisted the aid of his friends and family. In addition, he was able to make use of the crises in his life to achieve a "higher" form of health.

Later crises that Goethe encountered are symbolized by the figure of the poet Torquato Tasso in the play of the same name. Like Goethe himself on many occasions, the poet stares failure, mental and physical collapse in the face. His ambitions have been thwarted and he is spurned as a suitor. Tasso goes careering back and forth between projects of the utmost idealism and fits of offended dejection. He sees his magnificent house of cards come tumbling down and is increasingly tormented by the suspicion that he is nothing more than a figure of monumental ridicule. The only refuge he sees from pitiless mockery is to resort to a grandiose psychotic collapse. At that moment, the poetic word, the artistic vision comes to his rescue. As he puts it: "Where others fall mute in their torment, / A god has given me the power to say what I suffer."

Goethe's life and work were closely intertwined. Both of them were a constant succession of systole and diastole, tension and relaxation, a never-ending dialectic seesaw between proximity and distance, bounding elation and limitless self-pity. These are feelings that we all have to confront at various points in our lives. And Goethe's genius can provide us with a source of guidance in the labours of work and love, in our passage between night and day, passion and everyday partnership, sensory and aesthetic experience, and scientific rationality. In every human relationship we have to sustain the cooling of passionate ardour and learn to find new forms of potential development. This permanent process of "dying and becoming"—the banishment from the poetic picture gallery into empirical existence, there to find the foundations for new happiness—is subjected all our lives to the alternation of nascence and decay that is least painful and least likely to engender symptoms if we can actively accept it and build it into our little everyday world. Like no other poet, Goethe has shown the treasures our inner lives can bestow on us if we are able to keep happiness and sorrow alive. The poem "At Midnight" is an instance of the way in which Goethe is able to communicate this experience with the utmost cogency.

> At midnight I went, reluctant at that hour,
> A small, small boy, skirting the churchyard wide,
> To father's house, the vicar's, star on star
> And how they shone, all of them, how they shone,
> At midnight.

> When later then, and further in life's expanse,
> I needs must see my beloved, could not resist,
> Above me stars and northern lights a-clash,
> Going and coming I felt the selfsame bliss,
> At midnight.

> Until at last the light of the full moon
> Cut such a clear path in the darkness of my soul
> That my thoughts, made willing, supple, swift,
> Could encompass past and future all alike,
> At midnight.

The first stanza immediately appeals to the depths of our inner world. It recalls the fears and consolations of childhood. The brief "small, small boy" is suggestive of the halting heart-beat of the frightened child, while the churchyard reminds us of our dead. Then the overwhelming splendour of the firmament—and the overwhelming power of destiny that we will feel the brunt of sooner or later. But Goethe, the helpless, diminutive denizen of the earth, takes the liberty of finding this amazing power beautiful ("how they shone!"). Hubris? Perhaps, but also the courage to live on as best one can, to be whole, sound, healthy.

The poem illustrates how it is possible to be infant and adult at one and the same time and to the same degree. The poem is written both from the perspective of the small boy and from the distance afforded by Goethe's advanced age when he wrote it. Expressed in the phrase "reluctant at that hour", the psychic trauma of this child's life anticipates the discomfiture that Goethe was later to experience in the face of illness, exposure to fate, and death. The second stanza takes us out of the cosy familiarity of the family world. The blissfully remembered fields and banks may retain their resonance in "life's expanse" but there is also perhaps an element of menace. The beloved makes an appearance, standing for the yearning of flesh and blood. But she promises not only the bliss of satisfied desire but also the confusion of the heart. Cosmic powers are conjured—the stars and the moonshine—and we are privy to the bliss it signifies to feel as protected by one's own imagery as Goethe obviously was. Then the "coming and going" is not only tolerable but can also be actively pleasurable.

At the last, old age appears as the source of replete selfhood. The individual, for all his relative insignificance, can feel dignified and beautiful in harmony with the cosmos, as part of the grand design, when his thoughts and emotions "encompass past and future all alike".

Goethe's poem demonstrates how the child, the young man, and the wisdom of age can all live together and develop together. That which is past is not simply over and done with. It lives on in the present as a shaping force. This is why all talk of "phases of development" that we have to face, pass through, and then leave behind is foreshortened. Take the well-known phases posited by Freud. Throughout his or her life, every individual has an oral, anal, and phallic/genital world to structure. All of us have to find forms of expression for our symbiotic desires and narcissistic needs.

Goethe elevates this everyday perspective into the general sphere. In his autobiography *Literature and Truth*, he calls this subjective relation to the world "the sensation of past and present in one". My belief is that in the modern cult of the present we have much to learn from this sense of the historical within us.

As I have shown earlier, the relationship to what psychoanalysts call "internal objects" can be portrayed more graphically by artists than by scientists. But, like criticism in art, science serves to unravel what is not immediately accessible. Thus, when a scientist enters into a dialogue with a work of art, he may risk losing the visceral pleasure he took in it originally, but he may also emerge from the encounter enriched and enlightened. To further elucidate the hermeneutic and psychotherapeutic principles (memory, narrative shaping, interactional experience) in terms of the coherent experience of internal and external reality, I now turn to two works by Rainer Maria Rilke and Pablo Neruda.

Rainer Maria Rilke, a man of truly European culture, composed his *Duino Elegies* (1912–1922) over a number of years. The Chilean poet Pablo Neruda comes from a very different cultural background. He wrote his *20 Love Poems and a Song of Despair* in 1924, when he was barely twenty years old, in contrast to Rilke, whose *Duino Elegies* are a product of a poet at the height of his powers. But, for all these dissimilarities of origin, social situation, and life-style, the two poets articulate a message of very similar psychic verity: the actuality of experiences long since undergone and the presence of "archaic internal objects". These objects have to be confronted and coped with creatively, time and again.

Initially, Pablo Neruda's *20 Love Poems* appear to engage in an uninhibited celebration of physical love.

> Body of a woman, white hills, shining white thighs,
> you look like the world lying in surrender.
> My rough peasant body thrusts into you
> and makes the child leap from the depths of the earth.

After this breathtaking beginning and the brute glorification of sexual love, we are surprised at the doubts with which the first poem closes.

> Body of my woman, I will persist in your grace.
> My thirst, my limitless anguish, my path to the unknown!
> Dark river-beds where the eternal thirst flows,
> and weariness follows, and the infinite torment.

The second poem takes up this litany of torment, loneliness, and death, subjects that astound us in their contrast to the thrusting, erotic overture, and also in the face of what we know of Pablo Neruda's sensual nature.

> The light wraps you in its deathly flame.
> Abstracted pale mourner, standing there exposed . . .
> alone in the loneliness of this hour of the dead.

In the third poem the poet finds refuge once more in the vitality of the moment.

> In you the rivers sing and my soul takes flight in them,
> as you desire and where your wishes revolve.

Here, as in the "storm-laden morning" of the fourth poem, we have an insistent evocation of nature, the power of the wind that rages over the loving couple.

> It rages in the trees, divine, like an orchestra,
> like a language full of wars and anthems.

But the lyrical "I" finds no respite in this "flare-up" of sexuality.

> It bursts and expires as a mass of kisses,
> shattered on the gate of the summer wind.

The fifth poem introduces human language as a form of coping with terror and despair.

> And I see them far away from me, my words . . .
> They flee from my dark den . . .
> Once, they peopled the loneliness you now inhabit . . .
> That you hear them as I want you to hear me . . .
> The wind of fear still wrenches them from here to there . . .
> Be with me, my companion in this wave of fear.

The physical resonance of the beloved gives the lyrical voice a haven for its overwhelming feelings. Lonely words become language through the response of the beloved.

> But slowly my words take on the color of your love.

But what is the source of this pain, this profound fear? And what are these voices that interpose themselves in this young love?

> The wind of fear still wrenches them from here to there.
> Dream hurricanes cast them to the earth, sometimes.

> You hear other voices in my tormented voice,
> The sobbing of old mouths, the bleeding of old supplication.

What are these "old voices" that make themselves felt in the loving embrace? Here, Neruda appears to be visited by a very archaic form of fear. Behind what at first appears as an indefinite anguish we divine experiences with other people, "the sobbing of old mouths, the bleeding of old supplication". In an impressive concentration of images, Neruda evokes the urgings of unconscious figures concealed in this diffuse pain. The psychoanalyst will be reminded here of the early death of the poet's mother, an event that may well have left a profound wound that has never found expression in language. It could also be a primordial human experience, what Lacan calls a *"manque primordial"*, that is struggling to find verbal expression, the experience of being exposed to the night of existence with which we are all confronted, a darkness that we must fill with colour and life. Neruda shows us the way, escaping the black pit of fear by psychic representation and thus finding the path to life and love.

> Your picture in me is light, smoke, a pond as if asleep.

But this image has a depth that in its turn arouses the pain of old experience.

> You persist in darkness, woman, far from me and yet mine,
> from your gaze, on times, the coastline of horror rears up.

Here again, the poet apostrophizes figures (the "old mouths") that can generate a feeling of horror. With Melanie Klein, one might conjecture that these are the stirrings of objects that encroach upon us in loneliness and emptiness or, to use her terminology, "persecuting objects". To put it differently, we can see these as fragmentary elements of memory that have perhaps never attained consciousness, expressing themselves in the pace, rhythm, and physical affect aroused by the poem. Here too, the poet seeks a way out. As before, he finds it first in the erotic embrace, but this only affords response, acceptance, security for a limited period of time. Finally, the erotic encounter itself leads to horror and despair, as it does not engender a shared structuring of the world in language.

> I am the desperate, the word without echo,
> he who lost everything and he who possessed everything.

Neruda laments the wordlessness of the erotic encounter, the loneliness. In "long kisses" he senses "the death of the day turned thin". Immediately we have the raging, despairing resistance to loneliness and death in the sexual coupling.

> Moaning, flood of imprecation, tornado of crazed anger,
> rage over my heart, back and forth, without end.
> Wind from dead graves comes gorging, shatters,
> scatters your dreaming root.

The passionate attempt to escape the inimical "internal objects" is sustained by a longing for redemption.

> Ah, to follow the path that leads away from it all,
> where fear does not inhibit my step, not death, not winter
> with their open eyes through the dew of the morning.

In the twelfth poem, the poet recovers consolation and hope from the sexual embrace.

> For my heart your breast is enough, for your freedom my
>   flights.
> From my mouth what slumbered on your soul gains access to
>   heaven.

The beloved's responses bring release. They dispel loneliness and give the poet a home.

> Hospitable like an old path.
> You are peopled by echoes and voices of longing.
> I awoke, and sometimes there go winging away
> Birds that slept in your soul.

Loneliness, fear, and forgetting are resolved in a shared experience that makes it possible to sense the continuity of life. This experience is embedded in a larger historical context and in a spatial sense of belonging.

You are different from all others since I love you.
Let yourself be bedded by me on a litter of yellow garlands.
Who writes your name with letters of smoke
between the stars of the south?
Ah, let yourself remember how you were
when you did not yet exist.

Here again we have the time prior to remembrance, the motherly world, possibly intra-uterine, possibly the world as a condition of being sustained in cosmic religiosity. This unity is only established for a fleeting moment, soon "a strange shadow flits through your eyes". The beloved is once again remote; pain and the fear of death reassert themselves, only to be assuaged once more by verbal exchange and closeness.

I like you to be still, for then you are as if far away,
at one remove, marked by pain, as if you were in the grave.
Then all I need is a word, a smile, a small smile.
And I am happy, happy that you are with me.

Like a new tide coming after the ebb, the next poem brings back references to pain and death.

My heart springs to life on the yard of your death-black eyes.
In your sorrowful eyes the land of dreams begins.

Again and again we have the return of tormenting loneliness, remoteness, otherness, against which the loving embrace is no more than despairing resistance.

You are far away, further than anyone . . .
Your presence is alien, strange like a thing . . .
The sad rage, the cry, the loneliness of the sea.
Measureless, violent, twisted heavenwards . . .
So many sobs of passion, twined with my body . . .
Steeped in thought, burying lamps in deep loneliness.

In the eighteenth poem we have the culmination of the battle of pain and despair with the convulsive resistance of the erotic encounter. The longing for consolation and comfort in the arms of the beloved, the loved one as a haven, is destroyed over and over.

Sadder are the jetties when the haven heaves to.
And my life is consumed, senselessly tormented by hunger . . .
My satiety wrestles fiercely with turgid dusks.

Again the poet hymns the resplendent eyes and the smile of "light-flecked water", only to lament the inevitable and irrevocable loss of the beloved and of love in the twentieth poem.

How can the poet bear this profound pain? How can he live without the sureties of everyday life, without the protection of conventional rules and occupations that erect a sheltering fence against the abysses of love and death? Convention is a shelter for ordinary individuals, but at the price of making the daily round more intensive than artistic ecstasy. Let us ask once again how the poet can bear this? Patently through aesthetic shaping. It is here that he can sense and experience pain in all its profundity.

Tonight I can write the saddest verses.

In the *Song of Despair* the poet achieves personal accountability, he can renounce his beloved, separate himself from the woman who has given him so much pleasure, closeness, trust, while at the same time tormenting him with the excruciating longing for something that we can only grasp in religious or artistic terms. This "embracing embrace" with an "early mother" is anything but idyllic.

Oh, pit of debris, fierce cave full of shipwrecked!
In you, the wars and the flights accumulated.

But these horrors also afford beauty and freedom.

From you the wings of the songbirds took flight.
But danger still lurks.
You swallowed everything up, like distance.

It is a constant process of alternation.

It was the happy hour of assault and the kiss . . .
Turbulent drunkenness of love, in you everything sank!

The *Song of Despair* harks back to the injuries of childhood.

In the childhood mist my soul,
winged and wounded . . .

Finally, the poet evokes once more physical desire, ecstasy, despair. He copes with these feelings by finding a—his—language and thus comes to terms with pain, loneliness, and the fear of destruction. He finds hope for his future life and a path to his fellow human beings.

Rainer Maria Rilke's *Duino Elegies* come from a very different cultural background, tell of different personal experiences, and make use of different stylistic resources than Neruda's *20 Love Poems*. But they, too, revolve around similar psychic conflicts, "dark powers" concealed in erotic love and aesthetic experience.

For Rilke, the experience of holding out against suffering and pain was a necessary precondition for creativity. In exchanges and correspondence with Lou Andreas-Salomé, he enlarged on the links between the experience of suffering and the creative impulse. In letters to the friend of his youth, psychiatrist Viktor von Gebsattel, he explained his refusal of psychotherapeutic treatment with the fear of losing his creative powers as a result of recovering from his psychic sufferings. Before embarking on the *Duino Elegies*, Rilke felt despondent, down-at-heart, dejected. He wrote to Lou Andreas-Salomé saying that psychoanalysis would be too far-reaching a treatment for him. It would definitively help him to return to an orderly relationship with himself and for his creative powers this would be worse than the "utter disorder" in which he was living. For Rilke, a peaceful, healthy, ordered existence was incompatible with his work. He feared that the exorcism of the demons he was prey to would be synonymous with the banishment of the angels. The only treatment adequate to his condition was creative work. The Chilean psychiatrist and Rilke translator Otto Dörr Zegers (1996) sees this connection between suffering and creativity as a basic anthropological determination of the human condition.

Rilke begins his *Elegies* with the complete existential exposure of the human being to the aesthetic.

For the beautiful is nothing
but the awesome's beginning, which we barely endure,
and we admire it so, because it serenely disdains
to destroy us.

From a different vantage, Rilke then approaches the same topic as we found in Neruda: the dangers implicit in passionate love. And Rilke asks questions that are just as apparently mysterious as those of Neruda.

It is one thing to sing of the beloved. Another, alas,
to sing of that hidden, guilty river-god of the blood.

Like Neruda, he describes the loving encounter as conducive to the appearance of initially unknown internal figures normally hidden from our everyday experience. They

stir up the night to endless uproar.
And he himself as he lay relieved
under lulling lids of your gentle arranging
dissolving sweetness into the relish of fore-sleep:
he seemed protected . . . but *inside*: who warded off,
hindered inside him the tides of his origin?

As with Neruda, mothers, fathers, and other "internal objects" rear up in the loving embrace.

. . . loving
he descended to his elder blood, into the gorges
where terror lay, glutted with his ancestors. And every
awesomeness knew him, winked as if informed.
Yes, the horrible smiled . . . Seldom
have you smiled so tenderly, mother. How should
he not love it, since it smiled at him? Before you
he loved it, for when you were carrying him
it was dissolved in the water that buoys up the germinating one
. . .; not an individual child
but the forefathers who, like the rubble of mountains,
repose in our foundations; but the dry river-bed
of past mothers; but the entire
soundless landscape under cloudy or
clear fatality: this, girl, came before you.

This underlying dimension of the erotic encounter is initially a shock. Then comes the discovery of something consoling in the awareness of the mother, the mother who gave life to the poet,

a new being before briefly opened eyes.

It was the mother who soothed away the disquiet of the night and cooled his fever. But in his heart an abyss suddenly yawns, a terror that surprises us in view of the continuing presence of the mother's smile.

> . . . What
> women hated you then, what sinister men
> did you stir up in the veins of the youth? Dead
> children waited to find you.
> Console them gently
> with a simple daily task.
> Lead them into the garden, give them
> the dominion of night. Do not let them go.

What reveals itself here is an ambivalence between flight from these disturbing figures to everyday life and the longing to immerse oneself more completely in these ambiguous depths. How can the engagement with the "archaic objects" succeed? The answer is to give them shape and structure through language. This course even brings a reconciliation with death.

> But this: containing death,
> all death, even before life, so gently,
> and not being angry,
> is indescribable.

In everyday love and life, the deeper dimensions usually remain hidden, or else express themselves in diffuse moods. In poetry and passionate love they become tangible and find expression. But even then, happiness is always an anticipation of threatening loss.

> Oh not because happiness exists,
> that too-hasty advantage of a nearing loss . . .
> No, the pain and above all
> what weighs I the long experience of love,
> the inexpressible.

But this loss is something we can come to terms with by the use of language. It is here that we can find a home for ourselves.

> Here is the time of expressible things, here is their homeland.
> Speak and profess.

Language and artistic structuring make the threat of destiny bearable for us and it is sufficient for this experience to come about occasionally. Then, for all its sorrows, the self rises to extricate itself from the grasp of what threatens it.

> But should they awaken for us, the endless dead, a parable . . .
> And we, who conceive of *rising* happiness
> would be touched in a way
> that almost confounds us, when a happy thing *falls* . . .

In Rilke's poem, the intra-psychic shaping and structuring is condensed in the phrase "when a happy thing falls". The reference here is to language, communication, and love, but at the same time fulfilment and disappointment, presence and absence, the realization of Goethe's "die and become".

CHAPTER FOURTEEN

Summary

Counselling and psychotherapy are effective to the extent that they promote the creativity of clients or patients. Creativity is a life-style and a health resource. A creative life-style implies learning to be the authors of our own lives. A creative approach to our inner lives and our social environment gives us coherence and authenticity.

From modern practices of counselling and psychotherapy, psychoanalysis, hermeneutics, and creativity research, I have derived in this book principles that are of essential moment in many forms of counselling and therapy. It is in this sense that I speak of a *creative attitude*. It represents an integrative basis for the differential application of various counselling and treatment techniques.

Beyond that, in creative counselling and psychotherapy, hermeneutic principles are used as specific intervention strategies. In this way, professional and personal problems, psychic crises and disorders can be alleviated or removed altogether.

Creative counselling serves to assist in coping with distress and circumscribed conflicts by way of memory, narrative shaping, and interactional experience of the relationship of the client to him/herself and his/her social environment. Creative counselling encourages personal and professional development.

Creative psychotherapy is an aspect of psychodynamic and integrative therapies. The hermeneutic principles—memory, narrative shaping, interactional experience—are activated so as to remove certain psychopathological symptoms. Accordingly, psychic disorders can be successfully dealt with.

The creative hermeneutic principles of counselling and psychotherapy can be briefly summarized as follows:

Memory. An essential element in the counselling and treatment process is the acquisition of one's own personal history and access to the contemporary life-world by means of memory. Creative counselling and psychotherapy aims notably at overcoming a sense of alienation *vis-à-vis* individual and social experiences.

Narrative shaping. Overcoming alienation felt *vis-à-vis* internal and external experiences is achieved by means of systematic encouragement of creative potential. The structuring of initially diffuse internal perceptions by means of ideation, fantasy, and language creates the preconditions for coming to terms with pathogenic experiences.

Interactional experience. Narrative shaping makes initially alien events and processes susceptible of personal subjective experience. The job of the counsellor or therapist is first of all to structure emotionally relevant interactional events and processes on behalf of the client or patient. This structuring work and the interactional exchange of perspectives obviates the pathological virulence inherent in hitherto unstructured occurrences. Health is understood as a creative psychosocial development process.

These principles are implemented by means of three intervention strategies:

- competent empathy
- creative imagination
- interactive reflection.

The academic element in creative counselling and psychotherapy lies in the realization that psychosocial reality—real life and genuine subjective experience—cannot be adequately captured by technology and science. Meaningful counselling and effective psychotherapy are invariably products of understanding, in the fullest, most vital and practical sense of the term. As such they can point up routes towards successful communicative action and the art of socially responsible living.

REFERENCES

Assman, J. (2000). Schöpfungsmythen und Kreativitästskonzepte im Alten Ägypten. In: R. M. Holm-Hadulla (Ed.), *Kreativität*. Heidelberg/New York/Tokyo: Springer.

Adorno, Th. W. (1970). *Ästhetische Theorie*. Frankfurt: Suhrkamp. English edition, 1988. *Aesthetic Theory*. Minneapolis, MN: University of Minnesota Press.

Alexander, F. & French, T. M. (1946). *Psychoanalytic Therapy*. New York: Ronald Press.

Arieti, S. (1974). *Interpretation of Schizophrenia*. New York: Basic Books.

Balint, M. (1967). *The Doctor, his Patient and the Illness*. London: Churchill Livingston.

Balint, M., Ornstein, P. H., & Balint, E. (1973). *Focal Psychotherapy: An Example of Applied Psychoanalysis*. London: Tavistock Publications.

Bandura, A. (1982). Self efficacy mechanism in human agency. *American Psychologist*, 37: 122–147.

Baumgarten, A. G. (1741). *Texte zur Grundlegung der Ästhetik* [reprinted Hamburg: Meiner, 1983].

Beauchamp, T. L., & Childress, J. F. (1989). *Principles of Biomedical Ethics*. New York/Oxford: Oxford University Press.

Beck, A. T. (1976). *Cognitive Therapy and the Emotional Disorders*. New York: International Universities Press.

Blanchard, K., & Shula, D. (2000). *Everybody is a Coach*. New York: Harper Business.

Bion, W. (1962). *Learning from Experience*. London: Heinemann.

Bollas, C. (1992). *Being a Character*. London: Routledge.

Bowlby, J. (1988). *A Secure Base*. London: Routledge.

Caper, R. (1996). Play, experimentation and creativity. *International Journal of Psycho-analysis, 79*: 13–25

Crits-Christoph, P., & Barber, J. P. (2000). Long-term psychotherapy. In: C. R. Snyder & R. E. Ingram (Eds.), *Handbook of Psychological Change*, (pp. 455–473). New York: John Wiley.

Csikszentmihalyi, M. (1996). *Creativity. Flow and the Psychology of Discovery and Invention*. New York: Harper Collins.

Davanloo, H. (2001). *Intensive Short-Term Dynamic Psychotherapy*. New York: John Wiley & Sons.

Dewey, J. (1934). *Art as Experience*. New York: Minton, Balch [reprinted Carbondale and Edwardsville, Ill: Southern Illinois University Press, 1987].

Dilthey, W. (1900). *Einleitung in die Geisteswissenschaften*. Göttingen: Vandenhoeck & Ruprecht. English edition (1989) *Introduction to the Human Sciences*. Princeton: Princeton University Press.

Dörr-Zegers, O. (1996). *Espacio y Tiempo Vividos*. Santiago: Editorial Universitaria.

Eissler, K. R. (1963). *Goethe. A Psychoanalytic Study*. Detroit: Wayne State University Press.

Ellis, A. (1980). Rational–emotive therapy and cognitive behaviour therapy: similarities and differences. *Cognitive Therapy and Research, 4*, 325–340.

Emmelkamp, P. M. G. (2004). Behaviour therapy with adults. In: M. Lambert (Ed.), *Bergin and Garfield's Handbook of Psychotherapy and Behavior Change*, (5th edn) New York: John Wiley & Sons.

Felstiner, J. (1995). *Paul Celan: Poet, Survivor, Jew*. New Haven and London: Yale University Press.

Ferenczi, S., & Rank, O. (1924). *Entwicklungsziele der Psychoanalyse*. English edition (1986) *The Development of Psycho-Analysis*. Madison: International Universities Press.

Fölsing, A. (1995). *Albert Einstein*. Frankfurt: Suhrkamp

Frank, J. D., & Frank, J. (1991). *Persuasion and Healing* (3rd edn). Baltimore: The Johns Hopkins University Press.

Freud, S. (1895). The case of "Katharina". Studies on hysteria. *S.E., 2*: 125–134. London: Hogarth.

Freud, S. (1900). The interpretation of dreams. *S.E., 4*. London, Hogarth.

Freud, S. (1901). The psychopathology of life. *S.E., 6.* London, Hogarth.

Freud, S. (1905). Jokes and the relation to the unconscious. *S.E., 8.* (1960).

Freud, S. (1908a). "Civilized" sexual morals and modern neurotic illness. *S.E., 9.* London: Hogarth.

Freud, S. (1908b). Creative writers and day-dreaming. *S.E., 9*: 141–154. London: Hogarth.

Freud, S. (1910). On psycho-analysis. *S.E., 11.* London: Hogarth.

Freud, S. (1919). Advances in psycho-analytic therapy. *S.E., 17*: 159–168. London: Hogarth.

Freud, S. (1920): Beyond the pleasure principle. *S.E., 18.* London: Hogarth.

Freud, S. (1926). Inhibitions, symptoms and anxiety. *S.E., 20.* London: Hogarth.

Friedenthal, R. (1963). *Goethe. Sein Leben und seine Zeit.* Munich: Piper.

Gadamer, H. G. (1960). *Wahrheit und Methode.* Tübingen: Mohr. English edition (1989) *Truth and Method.* New York: Crossroad.

Gadamer, H. G. (1966) [1987]. *Apologie der Heilkunst. Ges. Werke Bd. IV.* Tübingen: Mohr.

Gadamer, H. G. (1976). *Philosophical Hermeneutics.* D. E. Linge (Transl. & Ed.). Berkeley: University of California Press.

Gadamer, H. G. (1986). *Hermeneutik II. Ges. Werke.* Tübingen, Mohr.

Gadamer, H. G. (1991). *The Relevance of the Beautiful.* Cambridge: Cambridge University Press.

Gadamer, H. G. (1996). *Die Kunst des Verstehens.* Cologne: Westdeutscher Rundfunk.

Goethe, J. W. von (1981). Gesammelte Werke. E. Trunz, (Ed.). Munich: Beck.

Habermas, J. (1971). *Theory of Communicative Action.* Boston: Beacon Press.

Hegel, G. F. W. (1807). *Phänomenologie des Geistes.* Bamberg: Goebhardt. English edition (1979) *Phenomenology of Spirit.* Oxford: Oxford University Press.

Hegel, G. F. W. (1812). *Schrifen zur Aesthetic.* Bamberg: Goebhardt. English edition (1998) *Aesthetic Theory.* Oxford: Oxford University Press.

Heidegger, M. (1923). *Sein und Zeit.* Tübingen: Mohr. English edition (1997) *Being and Time.* New York: State University of New York Press.

Holm-Hadulla, R. M. (1988). Structural links between schizophrenic disturbances of thinking and speech, paranoid experiences, and disordered intentionality. *Fortschritte Neurologie Psychiatrie, 56*: 1–7.

Holm-Hadulla, R. M. (1997). *Die Psychotherapeutische Kunst*. Göttingen: Vandenhoeck & Ruprecht.

Holm-Hadulla, R. M. (2003). Psychoanalysis as a creative act of shaping. *International Journal of Psychoanalysis, 84*: 1203–1220.

Horkheimer, M., & Adorno, T. W. (1944). *Dialektik der Aufklärung*. New York: Social Studies Association [reprinted as *Dialectic of Enlightenment* New York: Continuum, 1976].

Jauss, H. R. (1982). *Ästhetische Erfahrung und literarische Hermeneutik*. Frankfurt: Suhrkamp. English edition (1982) *Towards an Aesthetic of Reception*. Minneapolis, MN: University of Minnesota Press.

Kant, I. (1799). *Kritik der Urteilskraft*. Hamburg: Meiner. English edition (1934) *Critique of Judgement*. London and New York: Everyman's Library.

Kernberg, O. F. (1980). *Internal World and External Reality*. New York: Jason Aronson.

Klein, M. (1957). *Envy and Gratitude*. London: Hogarth Press.

Kohut, H. (1971). *The Analysis of the Self*. New York: International Universities Press.

Lacan, J. (1975). *Ecrits*. Paris: Editions du Seuil. English edition (2001) *Writings*. London: Routledge.

Lambert, M. J. (Ed.) (2004). *Bergin and Garfield's Handbook of Psychotherapy and Behavior Change* (5th edn). New York: John Wiley & Sons.

Langer, S. (1942). *Philosophy in a New Key. A Study in the Symbolism of Reason, Rite and Art*. Cambridge, MA: Harvard University Press.

Leuzinger-Bohleber, M. Stuhr, M., Rüger, U., & Beutel, M. (2001). Long-term effects of psychoanalysis and psychotherapy. *Psyche, 55*: 193–276.

Luborsky, L., Crits-Christoph, P., Mintz, J., & Auerbach, A. (1988). *Who Will Benefit from Psychotherapy?* New York: Basic Books

Mahler-Werfel, A. (1960). *Mein Leben*. Frankfurt: Fischer. English edition (2000) *Diaries*. Cornell University Press.

Meltzer, D. (1988). *The Apprehension of Beauty*. Worchester: Billing & Sons.

Malan, D. H. (1963). *Short-term Psychotherapy*. London: Tavistock.

Mann, J. (1973). *Time-Limited Psychotherapy*. Cambridge, MA: Harvard University Press.

Neruda, P. (1924). 20 poemas de amor y una canción de desesperada. Reprinted Madrid: Espasa-Calpe, 1997.

Obholzer, A. (Ed.) (1996). *The Unconscious at Work*. London: Routledge.

Parsons, M. (1999). The logic of play in psychoanalysis. *International Journal of Psycho-analysis, 80*: 871–884.

Philipps, J. (1996). Hermeneutics. *Philosophy, Psychiatry & Psychology*, 3: 21–28.

Proust, M. (1913–1927). *A la Recherche du Temps Perdu*. Paris: Gallimard. English edition (1996) *In Search of Lost Time*. New York, Vintage.

Racker, H. (1959). *Transferencia y Contratransferencia*. Buenos Aires: Paidós. *Transference and Countertransference*. Reprinted New York: International University Press, 2000.

Ricoeur, P. (1965). *De l'Interpretation*. Paris: Du Seuil. English edition (1981) *Hermeneutics and the Human Sciences*. Cambridge: Cambridge University Press.

Rilke, R. M. (1912–1922). Duineser Elegien. In: *Die Gedichte*. Frankfurt: Insel, 1987.

Rogers, C. R. (1957). *Client-Centered Therapy. Its current practice, implications and theory*. Boston: Houghton Mifflin.

Rose, G. J. (1996). *Necessary Illusion. Art as Witness*. Madison: International Universities Press.

Rorty, R. (2001). Universality and truth. In: R. B. Brandom (Ed.), *Rorty and His Critics* (pp. 1–30). Oxford: Blackwell.

Schafer, R. (1983). *The Analytic Attitude*. New York: Basic Books.

Schleiermacher, F. D. E. (1819–1825) [1984]. *Ästhetik*. Hamburg: Meiner.

Segal, H. (1991). *Dream, Phantasy and Art*. London and New York: Routledge.

Semprun, J. (1997). *L'écriture ou la vie*. Paris: Gallimard.

Stekel, W. (1938). *Techniques of Analytic Psychotherapy: Conditions of Nervous Anxiety and their Treatment*. Reprinted London: Routledge, 1999.

Stern, D. N. (1985). *The Interpersonal World of the Infant*. New York: Basic Books.

Strenger, C. (1991). *Between Hermeneutics and Science*. Madison: International Universities Press.

Sullivan, H. S. (1953). *The Interpersonal Theory of Psychiatry*. New York: Norton.

Valéry, P. (1854). *Cahiers*. Paris: Gallimard.

Walter, B. (1940). *Thema und Variationen*. Frankfurt: S. Fischer.

Weinrich, H. (1974). *Linguistik der Lüge*. Heidelberg: J. Groos.

Winnicott, D. W. (1971). *Playing and Reality*. London: Tavistock.

Wittgenstein, L. (1953). *Philosophical Investigations*. New York: Macmillan.

Yalom, I. D. (1980). *Existential Psychotherapy*. New York: Basic Books.